THE ROLE
of the CHIEF
EXECUTIVE

James Lines

BUSINESS BOOKS
COMMUNICA - EUROPA

First published 1978

ISBN 0 220 66355 6

This book has been set 11 on 12pt IBM Baskerville.
Printed by Thomson Litho Ltd., East Kilbride, Scotland.
Bound by Robert Hartnoll.
For the publishers, Business Books Limited,
24 Highbury Crescent, London N5.

Contents

Developing a management style — Consultation
and decision-making — Supporting subordinates
— Chief executive as long-stop — Trades unions
— Professional competence

Acknowledgements

I would like to express my thanks to Stanley Linden whose wide experience in industry and management consultancy has been of great help. He has suggested many of the themes of this book and also made a major contribution in reviewing and editing the first draft.

Also I would like to thank my wife who very seldom complained at my neglect of her and the children on weekends while I was writing.

James Lines

Introduction

The success or failure of any business depends on one man, the chief executive. Given enough time and freedom of action, he can turn a struggling second-rate company into a secure and thriving business — and *vice versa*. True, he cannot do it single-handed; but by his policy decisions, his choice of people, his determination, the quality of his decisions and his leadership, he can over-ride all other factors.

It is essential that he should be a good manager in the sense of running an efficient, technically competent organisation, able to meet tight schedules in a cost-effective way, with a cohesive management team. But to be a good manager is not enough; a chief executive must also be good at taking risks. Every policy decision involves some element of risk and every major step, such as the development of a new product, entry into a new market, acquisition of a new business, investment in new plant, has not only the possibility of providing an impetus to the business, but also of diverting it into what eventually may turn out to be a quicksand into which it may sink without trace.

Investigation and thorough planning can reduce the risk of error but cannot eliminate it. To try to opt out of the risk by minimising change is a short cut to stagnation and, therefore, is the biggest risk of all. Risk is, therefore, a basic feature of the job and a successful chief executive must be a good strategist and have his fair share of luck. He must also be ready to respond to events as they are — especially when they are not as he predicted them.

His skill is rather like that of the captain of an ocean racing yacht. He knows where he wants to go and has a rough idea of what weather to expect along the way; but there is no way in which he can plan a course and hold it regardless of the conditions about him. To win, he must react to every shift in wind and tide, be patient in the calms, survive a few storms without too much damage, and all without ever taking his mind off where he wants to arrive. His reactions must be precise; too little and all his alert competitors will slip past him, too much and he may well find himself going very fast in the wrong direction. Management at the top is much the same, although it is sometimes even harder to know what the wind and tide are doing.

It is impossible to deal in one book with all the multitudinous combinations of circumstances that chief executives face. What is more, even in a given situation, there are always too many unknown factors, not least of them the type of reaction one will get from the people one is dealing with. These unpredictabilities preclude the possibility of writing a book of recipes for every eventuality. All that one can do is to discuss the work of a chief executive as seen by an author with experience as a management consultant and a chief executive of a number of businesses, both large and small.

This book is intended for those who are responsible for the management of an autonomous business or who think that they will be in such a position in the course of their career. The former will know, and the latter must be warned, that there is no easy road to success. It cannot be found by reading a treatise on management. But a review of the key issues of a chief executive's job and a discussion of some of the solutions to his problems can help. This is what I have tried to do.

1 The Unique Role

When I first became a chief executive I felt that I understood
what the job was all about. As a successful manager and
management consultant I had watched chief executives at
work, sometimes with respect, often with friendship, but
also frequently with bewilderment. Why were they making
such obvious mistakes, adopting shortsighted policies,
sacrificing long-term objectives for short-term expediency,
promoting the wrong people? Above all, why were they failing
to get a grip on the situation, shake it up, and get the business
moving forward.

I saw the job just as an extension of any other executive
job, and I felt that the same management approach which
had served me well in the past would work again, even better,
because I would be unfettered by the constraints on my
freedom of action imposed by another man in that top job.

Essentially, I saw the job as one of introducing better
standards of management, running a tighter organisation,
applying more rigorous analysis and planning, adopting more
single-minded pursuit of objectives, than my predecessor; and
generally weeding out inefficiency.

I knew that the management team was in some disorder
and that the senior managers had their own ideas about how

the business should be run, and particularly about their own roles in it. There were disagreements about policy between them — not to mention clashes of personality and temperament. What is more, these were not young hopefuls, whom it was easy to override or overawe, but hardened professionals who wanted power and authority for themselves.

I had imagined that all that was needed was to say unequivocally what I wanted done, exert the authority of my position and, if necessary, bruise a few egos in the process. But it turned out that it was not as straightforward as I had expected. They knew what was going on in their departments and what the real problems were; I did not have anywhere near the same knowledge. Hence I had no choice in many cases but to rely on their advice. This was often conflicting and I had no way of knowing how much it was motivated by real concern for the welfare of the business and how much by personal ambition.

There was another problem too; with complete access to the accounts and other data, I rapidly came to the view that my previous priorities needed drastic revision. What was really wrong with the business was its fundamental market position; its products cost too much to make because too much labour and material had been designed into them. However efficient the current operation became, they could never provide an adequate financial return. The really urgent job I had to do was to reshape the product and marketing policies; efficiency was not the key issue.

I was finding out in practice what I had previously known only in theory. The role of the chief executive is by far the most demanding one in any organisation. Moreover, it is a unique role. All the other executive jobs are not only different in degree, they are also different in kind. The skills that a manager normally acquires as a middle-ranking and senior executive may well be relevant for the job of a chief executive, but they do not suffice. There are additional skills which the chief executive must have, which were often not required in his earlier career, or which were only of subsidiary importance. He comes to the job without necessarily having undergone a test in these skills. This is why many a successful deputy, when promoted to the top job, fails to make the grade in what should have been the climax of a distinguished career.

Job structure

The most obvious difference arises out of the comprehensive nature of the chief executive's responsibilities. His is a job whose job specification hardly needs to be written. It is basically the same in all businesses: he has the ultimate responsibility for the purposeful and profitable development of the company. He sets the objectives for the business and specifies strategies for their achievement. He initiates the preparation of the operational plans and has to make sure that these plans are being followed. He defines the organisational structure necessary to carry out the tasks he has identified and chooses the men who will fill the key roles in that structure.

He does not do these things in isolation, of course. If he is wise, he does them only after considerable discussion with his subordinates. But he alone is responsible for the performance of the business as a whole; he alone is accountable for its success or failure.

One of the difficulties in *discussing* the role of the chief executive is that it must of necessity be described in terms of such a structured pattern whilst the job itself is in fact very loosely structured. Theoretically it is possible to think of a logically related sequence of activities from setting objectives and making plans, devising a structure, selecting and appointing key executives, monitoring performance, collecting data on departures from plan, and so on. But in real life it is not like that at all. Almost every discussion and almost every decision involves aspects of policy, takes account of past achievement and future plans, has implications for company structure, and above all, modifies relationships between the individuals concerned. It is rarely possible to divide a problem into its facets and then consider each of them individually.

This is to some extent true of most executive jobs. But because most executives work *within* a framework of policy and structure which they may be able to influence to some extent, but which they cannot fundamentally change, they are able to narrow their focus much more closely. The chief executive, just because he is not constrained to the same degree, is much less able to isolate specific aspects of a problem. Frequently the overtones to a decision go far outside the implicit context and the decision-making process becomes that much more complex.

To illustrate this, let us assume that he has to appoint a new executive to head one of his production units. The personnel manager handling the appointment would be concerned to find a man to fit a given set of requirements. This may include the fact that the unit had a history which makes it necessary to have a man of a certain stamp, that the new man will have to deal with a group of executives who need to be handled with an amount of tact and diplomacy not usually thought of as being required in this type of post and so on. But the chief executive may view this appointment in the light of a number of purely speculative thoughts, which he is not ready even to hint at to his subordinates. For instance, he may be toying with the idea of making the unit the centre-piece of a new product division, or, on the contrary, of submerging it in another department; or he may feel that the appointment may be an opportunity to find somebody who could be trained to take over a key position in a revised organisation structure. Some of these thoughts may as yet not have been clearly enunciated or developed, but they will affect the picture he will form of the man required. This will then differ from that of the executive in charge of recruitment — and at the same time may be far vaguer, because of the alternatives jostling in his mind.

Relative freedom

Every executive in a business is working within an organisational framework and a system of strategic and operational plans which condition his objectives and priorities, constrain his freedom of action, but also limit his responsibility. The chief executive, however, has greater freedom of decisions and is much less bounded by such imposed constraints. This gives him an opportunity to develop the business in the direction be believes will result in an improvement of its performance. It also gives him the opportunity to make mistakes which may ultimately destroy it. It is this *relative* freedom to make or break a business which distinguishes the role of the chief executive from that of any other executive in the organisation. This is the essence of the role of the chief executive and, as has been said earlier, it is a situation for which his career up to then may not necessarily have prepared him.

Difference in kind

Unless the fates were particularly unkind, a person's first executive job would have been at a fairly low level in the organisation. At that level, the objectives of his job would be simple and clearcut, his tasks specific and his mistakes easy to identify. If his errors and omissions were to go undetected, their effect on the company's performance would not be very serious.

Usually, he will be working closely with a number of other executives and, as 'shop' is the inevitable small-talk of any social gathering in a business, he will have ample opportunity to hear his colleagues' views — whether he wants to or not. If he is not sure what to do in a given situation, he will be able to find out what his peers think. They may not know all the answers, but they might suggest solutions or make comments that will start him off on the path to a solution. Of course, young managers may resist seeking advice from colleagues, for one of the reasons for taking up management is to be able to make one's own decisions. But what then happens is that there is no specific request for advice. The problem is just 'kicked around a bit', say at lunch, and possible solutions emerge out of the general discussion.

If that does not work, he can always go to his boss. Whenever a junior manager runs into difficulties that he cannot resolve himself, or does not feel confident enough to make a decision, and goes for advice or instruction to his manager, the responsibility for the decision is taken from him. If he is an ambitious man, he may try to avoid referring his problems up the executive chain even more strongly than asking colleagues for advice. But in a well-run organisation he will be in frequent informal communication with his manager and will be discussing the more topical problems long before they reach the 'insoluble' phase.

A junior executive, therefore, usually works within a framework of relationships, which allow freedom of discussion with his colleagues, and in the confident knowledge that if anything arises that is too big for him to handle, he can pass it on.

Another characteristic of his work is that he is probably an expert in what he is doing. His department will have a relatively small range of specific tasks that he can get to know thoroughly. There is no reason why he cannot become familiar with every aspect of the operations of the limited number of systems and procedures within his department and be sensitive to all the influences affecting its smooth functioning. If he aspires to top management, this will probably be the last time in his career when he will have the comforting feeling of being thoroughly in control of things.

After a while, if the organisation is reasonably stable, he will discover his place in it, not just within the formal management structure, but in relation to executives on parallel line management paths, and to their subordinates and seniors. He will find that he has become a member of several interlinked working groups, within each of which his role will be intuitively understood by himself and by his colleagues.

For example, in the case of a manager of a small manufacturing department, one such group would be composed of himself and his immediate subordinates; another would consist of his own manager and that manager's other direct subordinates. Other groups could be based on the engineering department responsible for the development of the products made in his unit, or related to the quality management team; or the management accounting function, etc. In each of these groups he would have a varying amount of influence, depending not only on his formal relationships to them and his place in the structure, but also on the degree of respect felt for him and for his views by his colleagues within each group.

As he gains knowledge and experience and is given more senior appointments, this basic system of relationships will not change much. But his knowledge of the details of the work being carried out under his control may tend to diminish as his responsibilities widen and the consequences of errors of judgement will become more serious. However, he will still be able to discuss problems and opportunities with his colleagues before coming to decisions and he will also still be able to refer major issues to his senior and, indeed, will have the duty to do so if an issue is important enough.

When he becomes chief executive all this will change.

More responsibility, less knowledge

The first change is that his scope of responsibility is likely to increase four- or five-fold. If he has been controlling a single function, for example, he becomes responsible for all of them. This means that he will now know far less about the details of the work taking place under his control than he will have known at any earlier time in his career. Furthermore, there will be no possibility of his obtaining such a detailed understanding except in a small part of the business, and it would almost certainly be a misuse of his time to attempt to gain it.

Even if he decides to probe deeply into a problem area, the knowledge he can obtain will be superficial, because every situation has a time dimension only fully accessible to those working regularly within it. A man working within a department may well realise that, though certain aspects of the operations are unsatisfactory, he is making changes as fast as the department can cope. He may not be able to explain why he knows that the limits of rate of change have been reached; part of the reason may be a 'gut feel' about the ability of the people in the department to cope and their state of morale. As an outsider, a senior executive probing the department can never get the same understanding.

A chief executive, therefore, can never get to know in any

detail what is happening in his organisation and he must rely on information gathered, filtered and edited by others.

No equal colleagues

The second change is that he has no colleagues of equal status — only subordinates. If he has been promoted from within the company he may feel at first that his personal relationships with his erstwhile colleagues are unchanged. He may talk through situations, just as before, and listen to and respect their views, but he will soon realise that things have changed. His new subordinates will be more circumspect than they were before, more cautious about exposing their real thoughts, perhaps more wary because he now occupies a judgemental position and has the power to reward or dismiss. He will, therefore, soon recognise that although they may not have changed to him, he has certainly changed to them.

These changes in attitude will vary considerably from one individual to another, depending upon their personalities and abilities. Some may seek to ingratiate themselves; some will become more distant, erecting barriers of caution where none previously existed; some may become clamorous, seeking to influence him in the direction of their choice; the best, confident in their own ability, will change least, because integrity and intellectual honesty have their own absolute standards.

He may think it desirable to minimise this change in personal relationships; but, if he is to be effective, he cannot do so, because the reality has changed. It *is* his job to monitor and judge the performance of his subordinates. The real situation has changed and so must the interpersonal relationships that support it.

His colleagues will look to him for decisions and every one of them will have a differing view about every situation. Sometimes the differences will be extreme, sometimes minor, but some differences will always exist. It will be his job to examine the mass of relevant and irrelevant data, listen to advice, and decide what should be done; then, having decided, to make it happen. If he does that job well he will, to a greater or lesser degree, override all other views, and so create a distance — the distance of command.

Accountability

The third difference is that he has no organisational superior. He can no longer pass on any part of his responsibility. However successful he has been as a functional executive or as head of a smaller subsidiary unit, his major decisions then will have been tempered by the thought that they would have been known to his superior, who would have assessed them and, in extreme cases, changed them and who would, in the last resort, have accepted responsibility for them. The chief executive, if he is to be effective, must not attempt to refer his decisions elsewhere. He must make them, stand by them, and accept accountability for their outcome.

Even if the chief executive has the opportunity to discuss his problems with other people, such as the company's non-executive directors, he must not attempt to get them to share his responsibility for his decisions unless he wants to lose control rapidly. After all, if he invites them to take joint responsibility in one situation, he can hardly complain if they seek to intervene in other aspects of the business.

It is not, of course, suggested that the chief executive can be entirely free from constraints. The board of directors is ultimately responsible for the policies of a business and for its success or failure. It may see fit to impose policy decisions in considerable detail, or to require that a whole range of key decisions are referred to it before being implemented; but the degree of control which can be exercised from a board-room is different in degree and kind from the degree of control exercised at an executive level. The amount of discussion that can take place at a typical 2- or 3-hr monthly board meeting must necessarily differ from the prolonged and intensive examination within the company that would normally precede a major decision. This means that even the most interventionist board must leave a great deal to the chief executive.

In his relationship with his chairman and other non-executive directors, the chief executive must, therefore, tread a cautious path, referring policy matters to them, but with a firm positive recommendation when he does so. He must not refer to them decisions that are properly part of his managerial responsibility.

It will be obvious from what has been said about the role of a chief executive, as compared with other executive jobs, that both the pressure and the satisfaction can be greater. The pressure is greater because the chief executive knows that the whole future of the enterprise he is managing depends on the quality of his policies and decisions. Of course, luck plays its part and, as was the case with Napoleon's generals, one of the occupational requirements of a chief executive is to be lucky. But if things go badly, he cannot blame the state of the market, the economic situation, an unlucky combination of circumstances or any other of the myriad standard excuses for failure, he can only blame himself. So if things go badly, his is a very lonely position. If things go well the satisfaction is correspondingly intensified and his can be one of the most satisfying of occupations.

Summary

A chief executive is someone who, regardless of title, is responsible for the overall management of an enterprise. His role is a unique one. He alone has no colleagues, no seniors, only subordinates. He alone makes decisions that are not routinely monitored by some other executive. In the last resort he alone determines the success or failure of a business.

A chief executive may take on many responsibilities that have little to do with his real job. He may, for example, be a marketing man and be closely involved in the company's sales effort and the product range it offers. He may be primarily a financial expert, concerned mainly with the funding of the development of the business. He may be a technologist, concerned with keeping the company in the forefront of its particular field of technical expertise. Indeed, in the case of most small businesses, it is highly likely that the chief executive will have some such involvement, because businesses grow initially out of such specific skills. But once a company has outgrown this phase, he will not have the time to be the company's chief salesman or designer or any other functional specialist. He will then have to concentrate on his primary role, which is made up of three related responsibilities:

1   To establish an overall plan for the development of the business.
2   To select the key subordinates and organise them in the most effective pattern to achieve the objectives of the plan.
3   To monitor and control their activities to ensure that the objectives of the plan are achieved.

These three elements of planning, delegation and control are absolutes. If the chief executive carries out these responsibilities well, then most of the other things that he does become matters of secondary importance.

Of course, these three aspects encompass a great deal and require considerable knowledge, experience and ability to perform them effectively. Each of these responsibilities and requirements will be discussed in some detail in the following chapters.

2 Strategic Plans and Objectives

Small companies can exist quite well without written strategic plans and without any overt objectives. They react to changing external circumstances by making minor adjustments to the way in which they operate, and take what their managers deem to be good opportunities as they occur. Successful innovations are retained and become part of normal business practice and the unsuccessful ones are quietly dropped.

Such companies, drifting on the tide of economic affairs, surviving in this way as best they can, are probably in the majority. Their development parallels the evolutionary process in nature. Some adapt, survive and prosper; others fail to adapt, or do so too slowly, and are extinguished by competitive forces. During times when business conditions are relatively stable, the process of change is also relatively slow, so that such companies tend to grow or decline relatively slowly. In periods of rapid economic change some of these businesses may find themselves in a benign environment for their particular strengths and, therefore, grow quickly; others enter a sudden decline. Even the ones that are well suited to the new environment may encounter secondary problems and fail to cope with the organisational and financial problems of growth.

12

One of the reasons why this system (or really lack of system) can work reasonably well in a small company is that the chief executive is able to be personally involved in almost everything that is going on, and take quick corrective action if the company appears to be running into problems. With a small company, the effect of such action itself is generally rapid enough to safeguard the company's future.

It is often incorrect to say that such small companies have no strategic plan. The absence of a set of formal, written objectives may make it appear that they are not pursuing any clearly identifiable aims. But in truth, there may be quite a detailed plan firmly lodged in the chief executive's head. What is more, the chief executive, being constantly around, may communicate and hammer home his plans and hopes, his strategies and wishes, to his subordinates quite effectively.

But unless the man is a genius, there must come a point in the development of a business where this 'system' will break down. Things will become too complicated, particularly if there are several product ranges, disparate markets, disparate technologies, etc. Above all, size will in the end make this type of management by personal touch impracticable.

For in a large business the chief executive cannot know what is going on in all parts of the company. And when things start to go wrong it takes longer for the decline to become obvious and corrective decisions are slow to take effect, so that any form of setback can be relatively much more serious in terms of company survival.

Need for a defined strategy

Even in a small company, a systematic attempt to forecast future trends and to develop a business strategy to take best advantage of them, will materially improve performance and make unforeseen disaster less probable.

In the case of a large company it is essential that the chief executive should operate according to a written strategic plan and to published objectives. Such a plan is an attempt to foresee the outcome of technical, market and economic trends and to use them to the best advantage. The fundamental assumptions will not always be right, but provided that the basic plan is flexible and is supported by adequate contingency plans, a company that operates such procedures is likely to grow faster, and resist adverse economic conditions more effectively, than a company that does not adopt a process of strategic planning.

A formal strategic plan determines the purpose of the company's operational plans and, therefore, gives an overall unity to its operations. This unity is important, not only because of the need to avoid the impossible task of having to implement conflicting programmes, but also as a motivating force. Managers like and need to work as part of a group which has an overt and accepted set of objectives, from the achievement of which they can take satisfaction.

The chief executive may also find the process of preparing the objectives helpful in itself. He may think that he already knows how he wants his business to develop, but having to think about it with sufficient clarity to prepare a formal plan can be a great aid in focusing attention on the matters of greatest importance to success.

A quotation, which was alleged to have appeared on the notice board of a major American corporation during a time of business difficulty, said: 'When you are up to your arse in alligators, it is not easy to remind yourself that the reason you went into the swamp in the first place was to drain it'. A chief executive can easily fall into the temptation to spend his time shooting alligators rather than draining the swamp; so it helps to have written reminders of the real priorities.

The chief executive will be aware, however, that a set of objectives could be a two-edged weapon. If business targets are too easily achieved, they can be as demotivating as when they are too difficult to achieve. He will, therefore, be striving for a balance between objectives that are sufficiently difficult to stretch himself and his subordinates, but not so difficult that their achievement is an unlikely outcome of such efforts. This is a balance easy to express but not easy to achieve in practice.

Link between objectives and plan

Setting objectives, and developing a strategic plan for their achievement, are such interlined activities that they can be regarded as twin outcomes of the same management process.

In theory, it is possible to set general financial objectives and then, as a separate process, develop business strategies to enable the objectives to be achieved. But this is an artificial division, because objectives defined without considering the means by which they are to be achieved are merely expressions of hope and hardly worth the name 'objectives' at all. On the other hand, to formulate a strategic plan without thinking out beforehand where the plan is intended to lead is also likely to be an unproductive exercise. It is not possible, therefore, to state whether the setting of objectives or the strategic planning should have priority, but to regard them as related, mutually interacting activities.

This is, of course, a very common aspect of management. Management decisions are very rarely reached through a logical progress from well-founded assumptions to inescapable conclusions. Instead they are rather the result of the impact of a multiplicity of influences and, in many cases, a matter of personal judgement rather than of objective knowledge.

That is one of the reasons why most planning processes are reiterative. A plan is prepared with some very general objectives in mind; when the plan has been evaluated it is found that it would not produce the required outcome; the objectives are re-examined and possibly modified; changes are made to the plan. This goes on until, eventually, a plan is derived which seems to provide an acceptable outcome to all parties. This can then be formulated into a set of formal objectives.

Purists may claim that any set of objectives will include a target rate of return on capital employed and of growth of assets, and these objectives, among others, are independent of the nature of the business, but derived directly from the cost of funding, shareholders' aspirations, or some other general factors.

It is undoubtly true that the rate of interest paid for borrowed capital is a crucial factor in assessing the required rate of return on that capital, particularly in a company with a highly geared financial structure. But even in the case of general financial factors it serves no useful purpose to quantify them as objectives without consideration of the company's strategic plan.

For example, if the strategic plan entails rapid growth, it may be necessary to enter new markets and initially incur losses to penetrate those markets. In such a case, there may be a deliberate intention to accept a reduced rate of return on the company's capital until the position in the new markets is fully established. A low rate of return on capital employed, for several years, might well be a direct outcome of such a planned growth strategy. To set as a primary objective just a high rate of return on capital employed might well inhibit the growth essential for a company's longer-term success. It is, therefore, by no means an unusual decision to sacrifice short-term profitability in pursuit of longer-term goals. However, if this is proposed, the chief executive may well find himself in conflict with the company's owners or shareholders, who may not be in a position to judge directly the company's business environment and may not be willing to accept deferred success, but require a higher income immediately. It is, therefore, necessary to compromise between short- and long-term consideration.

Individual managers within the business will also have assessed what progress can be expected in their operating units, profit centres or functions, and the sum total of their forecasts is quite likely to be at variance with the objectives derived from shareholders' expectations and from the chief executive's strategic thinking.

There are, therefore, many influences on the planning process, and often inescapable conflicts between what the chief executive believes can be achieved, what his subordinates consider is possible, and what he knows the board of directors would wish to see achieved.

Evolution not revolution

A major influence on the planning process is the company's

history. A company can change only slowly, almost regardless of the pressures that are brought to bear on it. Indeed, extreme pressure for change can have a negative effect; pressure always generates opposition, and also rapid change may disorient long-serving and loyal executives. For reasons of this kind, any objectives that are not a direct outcome of the application of a company's existing strengths are likely to be missed by a wide margin.

It is a primary contention, therefore, that a company's objectives and its strategic plan are both heavily dependent upon the company's past performance and existing strengths. This may seem quite obvious, but experience shows that many companies set objectives which manifestly do not fall within the scope of their existing strengths. This may happen because the executives concerned have a mistaken idea about the source of their own company's success, and try to apply strengths that are only there in the company mythology, but not in real life. It may also happen because of the common experience that every other businessman's problems seem much easier than one's own. His markets are more stable, his competition less fierce and his opportunities more obvious.

There can, therefore, be a temptation to change the course of a company's development in a dramatic way in order to take up an apparently attractive new opportunity. Many companies run into trouble in the attempt, first, because the new field usually turns out to have just as many problems as the original one and, secondly, because the company has moved into a situation in which its distinctive competence may no longer be relevant.

Distinctive competence

No business is good at everything. Not very long ago when conglomerates were fashionable, some entrepreneurs claimed that they could run any business successfully because of an abstraction called 'management skill'. Some of those businesses are no longer in existence, and the conglomerate idea has lost a great deal of its appeal. One of the reasons for this is that the management formula of so many of them — cut back inventories, institute strong cash-collection procedures, sell off the surplus assets, trim the overheads, weed out the unprofitable products, rationalise the product range — is essentially a defensive one.

Creative actions require a great deal more than just this type of management skill. They require a thorough understanding of the basic characteristics of a business and of the markets in which it operates. It is a complex relationship which is difficult to understand without specific experience, and even more difficult to change, and yet it is the foundation upon which any strategic plan has to be built.

In dealing with its external environment, every business has a unique mixture of strengths and weaknesses; the balance between them is the factor that has determined the level of its past success. As all except small businesses are relatively slow to change in any fundamental way, a strategic plan is more likely to be successful if it is based on the development of existing strengths, rather than on the injection of new ones, or just by remedying weaknesses.

The first step in developing a strategic plan is, therefore, to examine the business with considerable care and objectivity, with the intention of identifying the strengths that are to be the foundation of its future development. In essence it is a matter of saying: 'These are the things we are good at now. If we concentrate on applying these abilities, where would that lead us in the future?'

It is not, of course, suggested that a company's weaknesses should be neglected, or that the introduction of new skills is not a proper part of business development. Far from it. The correction of identified weaknesses should have a prominent part in the business plan. But changing a company's fundamental character is a long and arduous process, and to base a plan on the assumption that this can be done painlessly and quickly can lead to the waste of a great deal of management effort without much to show for it.

The primary strategy, therefore, should depend on existing strengths; remedying weaknesses and the development of new forms of competence should be secondary factors in the business plan.

The distinctive competence of a business may not be

readily apparent to those who work within it, unless they deliberately stand back and take a fresh look. This entails asking some fundamental and searching questions, not only of executives within the business but of customers and suppliers.

In practice, if the chief executive has been with his business for any length of time, he will already have well-formed ideas about the strengths and weaknesses of the business, but when he asks his senior executives, he may be surprised to find that their views are very different. He may be convinced that the company owes its success to his astute financial management coupled with an entrepreneurial grasp of market needs, his senior engineering executives may put it all down to superior product quality, the marketing staff, on the other hand, may discount his entrepreneurial flair and point to their own professional competence.

One thing the chief executive could do is to initiate a market research project to find out why the company's products are purchased in preference to those of its competitors, and why they occupy a particular place in the market. But if he is not already engaged in regular customer contact, perhaps the best thing to do is for him to visit a number of customers himself. If he goes prepared to talk very little and listen a great deal, he will find out much about his company that was previously unknown to him. He will certainly learn about the things that are going wrong; then, after the criticisms, he will hear the praise — the reasons why his company holds its market position. For example:

> Your sales force are not very well trained. They don't know enough about your products, and you don't give them enough advertising support, but your products are reliable. When we sell them we know they won't come back.

> It is pre-sales service that sells your products. Your applications engineers work very closely with our design department, so that your components are designed into our products from the start. In themselves they are not much better or worse than others available on the market.

19

Your company had a wonderful reputation once and are still living on it. You are being overtaken very rapidly by competitors who are offering better products at lower prices. Your brand reputation may carry you on for a bit longer.

The answers will not be even remotely uniform. Regional differences, local situation, the nature of a particular customer's needs, personal idiosyncrasies, and many other influences will condition the responses, including any problems affecting the most recent transaction. But there is likely to be a central core of agreement that will provide a valid picture of the customer view-point.

Similarly, within the company, frank and detailed discussion, involving all the company's senior executives will reveal the sources of its strength. It may reside in just one or two individuals; it may be design skill, or a flair for judging what customers will be buying next year, it may be technological strength that leads to high product reliability — or a very well-equipped tool room may ensure that engineering components are more than usually precise and so permit a very high standard of quality control to be applied to the final product without causing excessive assembly and rectification cost.

The answers may emerge at a number of levels. For example, customers may buy the products because of their reliability, which may arise from stringent quality control, which in turn may be the result of conservative engineering standards — a slow rate of innovation may turn out to be a source of business strength. If this seems to be a paradox, it is nevertheless not untypical. The generally accepted fields of competence may prove to be either inadequately distinctive or not the real source of the strength of the business at all.

A company producing industrial chemicals wrongly believed that its very creditable performance was based on the technological strengths provided by its research laboratory. At a time of shortage of funds, it was cutting back the relative level of its sales force so as to be able to fund an expansion of its laboratory in order to diversify into new materials. In fact, its performance was very largely due to the deep technical understanding of its field representatives, and the relationship that they had built up with customers. To reduce that sales force was probably one of the most damaging things that could have been done to that company.

In another case, a company operating in boom conditions thought that its ultimate strength lay in its product quality and assumed that, when the boom ended, its manufacturing programme could be sustained by an increase in market share arising from its product reputation. In practice, its reputation had been gained many years earlier, but had faded partly because the efforts to expand production to keep pace with market growth had resulted in several quality crises. When the boom ended, far from increasing its market share, it lost heavily. In this case the company mismanaged the source of its strength, but believed wrongly that the strength endured.

The first step in strategic planning is, therefore, for the chief executive to examine the company's past and present operating situation and to consider very carefully the mainsprings of its success. He will obviously consult his senior executives and, hopefully, come to a conclusion to which they can all subscribe. But he must be sure that the conclusion is one that he personally endorses, because to be wrong at this stage is to be wrong in everything that follows.

Shareholders' aspirations

A further factor to be taken into account before the planning process starts is the pressure and constraints applied by the company's owners.

If the company is a subsidiary of a large corporation there may be widespread limitations on the freedom with which the chief executive can change the nature of the existing business. For example, there may be other subsidiary companies operating in adjacent fields of business, whose existence limits opportunities for lateral diversification. There may be specific criteria applied to new funding, a defined level of return on new capital, or the requirement that a certain proportion of new funds should be internally generated. There will almost certainly be a target rate of return on all the assets employed by the company, and perhaps other key ratios may be under surveillance.

If the company is independent there will probably be fewer guidelines but the availability of funds will certainly be a limiting factor. Usually there are several degrees of limitation, depending upon the nature of the investment and the projected return; so the constraint is usually conditional rather than an absolute one.

The chief executive may also be confronted with the need to take defensive actions against possible acquisition by a third party. This may have a considerable bearing upon his attitude to the balance between short- or long-term return on investment.

Economic trends

A third major influence on the strategic plan is an assessment of market opportunities. Since we are considering a *strategic* plan this will normally be a matter of considering general economic trends and the influence of such trends on the markets within which the company is operating (or potentially could be operating).

Well-run companies will have a continuous input of the economic information relative to their markets, and will be monitoring trends by the examination of published data. For each of the main facets of the company's business it is worth preparing a summary of such information. This serves to ensure that basic economic assumptions have been explicitly considered and are exposed for critical comment. If this is not done explicitly, there is a danger that what 'everybody knows' about a particular market may turn out later to be one man's opinion vigorously expressed with which almost everyone else disagrees.

I do not believe that strategic planning is basically the result of the applications of convergent logical thought to the observed and forecast trends. There are too many discontinuities in business life for that to be true, but any plan that ignores the basic economic trends is founded on quicksands and will collapse, however elegant its architecture. So, if such economic data is not already available, then it must be obtained. Most of what is needed for strategic planning can be obtained by desk research which need not be expensive.

It is worth, perhaps, repeating here what has been suggested earlier, that no assumptions are sacrosanct, whoever has formulated them, including the chief executive himself. No one has a monopoly of wisdom about the future and, in too many situations, the chief executive leads his company into trouble because his own subordinates are not willing or permitted to tell him when they think he is wrong. It is a basic principle that there must be free discussion at each stage in the planning cycle. No one should use positional authority in order to substantiate an opinion.

Of course, at the end of the discussion, a decision has to be made, and that is an entirely different matter. The decision must be made by the executive who will be held accountable for that particular part of the plan — the chief executive in the case of major issues.

Technological considerations

Technological trends and discontinuities also have to be taken into account and their effect on the future of the business assessed. The trends are usually not difficult to handle in industries where a discernable movement is taking place. In consumer electronics, for example, there is a swing towards integrated circuits and a steady reduction of the real cost of providing a certain functional performance, which carries the implication that a given factory area and labour force will steadily increase its real unit output for that reason alone. This, in turn, leads to a need to plan for expanding sales for existing products, or for the disposal of surplus capacity by product diversification, or perhaps by contracting the scale of manufacturing operations.

Technological discontinuities are much harder to identify in advance. One good example is the change in design of truck-mounted cranes. About 10 years ago they would all have had lattice jibs, carried in sections and assembled on site. Five years later almost all would have had telescopic cantilever jibs, the real change having taken place over about two years. The effect was dramatic for the companies involved, because their whole design and manufacturing technology had to change and a substantial amount of retraining was required. In that particular case it is hard to say to what extent the change could have been predicted. With hindsight, the availability of suitable grades of high tensile steel and the use of box girders for other applications — bridges for example — were indicators, but they were not necessarily obvious pointers at the time.

Preparing an outline plan

When the groundwork has been completed, the general requirement of the company's owners are known, its distinctive competence has been identified and general economic and market circumstances have been assessed, it becomes possible to start the real planning process.

Generally the first stage is to put together some speculative assumptions about the directions in which the company might develop.

I have always found that this is one job that the chief executive can do best himself. He is now doing some very basic thinking about the future development of his business, and that comes very close to the heart of his responsibilities.

The chief executive has on his desk:

1   An analysis of the company's existing competence.
2   A review of likely economic trends in the company's main markets.
3   An analysis of the likely technical trends affecting the products and markets.
4   A summary of the general objectives of the company's owners, shareholders, etc.
5   Any earlier strategic plans.

His job is to consider the options open to the company in terms of its future development.

Normally there will be a series of overlapping possibilities. They will include routine developments in existing fields of business and the possibility of increasing the existing market share (although usually there will be more than one way to achieve each of these).

There will be a whole range of conditional opportunities. For example, a plan to grow by acquisition may depend to a very large extent upon a suitable purchase being available at the appropriate time. It may be decided to enter a new market; but until a market study has been carried out, it may not be possible to decide whether this should be through local distributors or a direct sales force. There may be even more speculative possibilities — perhaps the need to move out of certain declining areas, while still having only a very general definition of the characteristics of the new product ranges required, but no certainty that they can be successfully developed.

It is almost certain that the range of possibilities will be too large for any but a very superficial analysis of most of them. It is, therefore, necessary for the chief executive to select for further evaluation a few combinations of the possibilities available. It is often convenient to write down these selected programmes in the form of working scenario or outline plan.

It may seem objectionable that the chief executive should draw up a scenario after a relatively superficial assessment of some of the possibilities. I believe that this is justified, if only because of the sheer impossibility of examining all possibilities in depth. It is also my experience that, provided the selection of policies is done with reasonable competence, business success arises as much from having a consistent policy and carrying it out well, than from particular brilliance in selecting the policy in the first place.

The chief executive will, therefore, prepare a scenario for future company development. The scenario will contain much that is reasonably firm and generally accepted, being a natural extension of existing policies, as well as proposals for developments which represent new initiatives for the business.

A typical scenario would discuss the main markets in which the company is currently trading, and the trends affecting them, describe the proposed marketing and product policies and forecast the company's market share and total volume of sales in each market. It will outline plans for the development or rationalisation of the product range. If the chosen policy entails the acquisition of other businesses, or joint ventures, the scenario will discuss how the partners are to be identified and how the ventures will be financed.

Similarly, other elements of the strategy will be woven into the scenario; the size of the expected cash flows and profit returns will be assessed.

It is likely that the scenario or outline plan will consist of a number of elements of varying degrees of reliability. The main direction of business development may not be in doubt, but in some areas there may be alternative development programmes depending on issues which cannot be resolved at the planning stage. A typical example of such uncertainty would be the case of a company planning growth through an acquisition programme. In the case of a retail business, a programme to acquire a planned number of new branches each year would be credible as a firm plan, because the requirement would be likely to be a small proportion of the total number of retail stores available for purchase at any one time. If, however, the target acquisition was one of a small number of manufacturers in a specific field, then the probability of one of them being freely available for sale would be relatively low and successful acquisition would, therefore, depend on specific negotiations. Clearly, in the first case there can be a firm plan and in the second case there can only be what amounts to a statement of intent.

Another example of conditional planning might arise from the intention to develop a new market overseas. A company might deduce from general economic factors that there are great opportunities for its products in a specific territory. The outline plan might, therefore, specify that the market should be investigated with a view to building an export business there. In practice, when each of the separate regional markets in the area is investigated it may be found that the company's products are not as suitable as was originally envisaged, which may mean that the project has to be abandoned or that new products have to be developed. It may be that an original view that the market could be exploited through a local distribution agent has to be changed, and the company may need its own sales force in the area in order to penetrate the market successfully.

Uncertainties of this kind, which are characteristic features of strategic planning, are often given as an excuse for not preparing long-range plans at all. In practice uncertainty, although inevitable, affects only a small part of the total plan. In any case, to have to express a general intention, to outline a decision tree, to decide how and when the first level of questions are to be answered, ensures that matters are considered more thoroughly, more logically and more positively than would be the case without a plan.

It is this outline which, after several stages of reiteration, will be turned into a strategic plan and a set of key objectives.

Having reached the outline plan it is then possible for the chief executive to say to each of his key subordinates: 'Within the framework of this outline plan, prepare strategic plans for your own operating unit, identify the capital and human resources required, specify any key problems which might affect the achievement of the plan, and assess the financial outcome'.

While this is being done, there will certainly be an almost continuous dialogue between the chief executive and the heads of the main operating units, to clarify differences in interpretation, and to resolve a whole range of practical questions that will arise. Eventually each of the operating units will have prepared its own plan, and these plans can then be consolidated by the chief executive or his corporate planner into a company-wide plan. The consequences of following the plan, in terms of the main financial parameters — capital, profitability, cash flow, funding — can then be evaluated. If the projected outcome is considered satisfactory in terms of the known constraints on the business, the plan can be formalised by publishing a set of business objectives at company and operational levels. But, more often than not, the forecast results will not be considered acceptable, and the outline plan will be amended in the light of the additional information that has emerged from the planning round and the process is repeated. There can be several stages of reiteration until a plan that does seem to provide an acceptable outcome is finally developed.

The use of a corporate planning department

Within a small company the chief executive will not only initiate the strategic planning process, but he himself will also almost certainly have to reconcile the individual departmental plans and the company plan, and convert them into operating plans.

In the case of a larger company a corporate planning department will usually deal with these matters. For this to work successfully, however, it is essential that the chief executive should regard it as an extension of his own personal responsibility, rather than a separate function of management. The corporate planning staff should be deeply involved in the business; they should discuss with the heads of the operating units their opportunities and problems and work with them in resolving the various uncertainties. They must become accepted contributors at each planning level. Any suggestion of sitting in an ivory tower will nullify their value to the chief executive in his planning function.

If I may push an earlier analogy a little further, building a strategic plan is somewhat like the task of an architect designing an important new building. He needs to assemble all the available information about the uses to which the building is likely to be put — the underlying geological strata, the funds available, the tastes of his clients, etc. — and unless he is thorough in doing this, the building, however elegant, is likely to be a failure. But the actual design comes from his personal feeling and judgement. He will probably try a few basic layout plans, but he cannot possibly try all the possibilities, nor can he be sure that, when the detailed planning takes place, his general design will not require modification. If the end-result is to be effective and satisfying, it must be the creation of one man's imagination and judgement. It cannot just be logically functional. It cannot be the work of a design committee.

Similarly, business planning is not entirely or even primarily a reasoning process. It consists of a series of judgements made on the basis of experience, in a constantly changing environment in which competitors are actively planning to improve their own position. The most important

28

ingredient here is the quality of judgement, not the quality of intellect, and the only way a corporate planner can sharpen that judgement is to become involved in the real problems of the business and their day-to-day outcome.

The outcome of the planning process

Typically, the outcome of the strategic planning process will be a five-year plan for the company. (The period, of course, could be considerably longer in the case of heavy industry, for example.) It will probably include a descriptive outline of the way in which the company is expected to develop over each of the coming five years.

The plan will include:

1   A review of each of the markets in which the company will operate, setting out their main characteristics as far as they relate to the product or the service under review.
2   A definition of the outline marketing strategy in each market segment at which the company's products and services are directed, including an assessment of the planned market share for each of the periods under consideration.
3   A review of the company's product range and a general plan for the replacement of obsolescent products and the development of the range to meet the anticipated market needs.
4   A definition of the sources of products and the main decisions about in-house manufacture or external purchase.
5   A forecast of the resources required to implement the strategic plan, including human resources, and a plan for their generation.
6   A statement of any planned major investments, showing their projected timing and effect.
7   A plan for divestment or closure of any activities that no longer contribute to the selected objectives.
8   The outcome for the company in terms of the key financial variables — capital, profit, cash flow, funding.

Objectives

Any strategic plan will necessarily include a wide range of implicit and explicit objectives. Typical of these would be such factors as market share, dates of introduction of products into particular markets, establishment of a new manufacturing facility, development of a new product range and, of course, the achievement of the planned profit and cash flow. Some of the objectives will be of secondary importance or conditional on a particular way of carrying out the intentions of the strategic plan, while others will represent the essence of what the company is trying to achieve.

It is helpful to identify and tabulate objectives of the latter kind which can then be published to act as milestones against which the company's progress can be measured. Normally they will consist of two kinds of factors: key dates by which certain events will have taken place, and levels of achievement during specified future periods. The publication of these helps to focus management attention on those aspects of the plan that are fundamental compared with those that are merely descriptive or conditional.

In addition it is necessary to select objectives for each major department or function within the company. These need to be selected so as to ensure that their achievement would virtually ensure that the company's overall strategic plan would be achieved. Clearly the way in which the company is organised has a considerable bearing on the selection of these objectives, but equally consideration of the crucial elements in achieving the strategic plan should lead to consideration of the company's organisational structure.

It is desirable that the achievement of each major objective should be the responsibility of a single executive, and that he should have within his control the resources necessary to achieve it. Only by such an arrangement can effective delegation be carried out.

The strategic plan, the selection of objectives and the structure of the company are, therefore, closely intertwined elements of the same planning and reasoning process. This is dealt with more fully in the following chapters.

Investment decisions

All major investments need to be in response to meeting the
objectives of the strategic plan. There is a tendency in some
companies to try to work out a financial justification for
such investments in isolation. But in my view this is rarely a
realistic approach. Many of the effects of an investment may
be difficult to isolate, so that it may be judged on too narrow
a basis. Consider the example, discussed earlier, of a company
investing in an overseas agency. Some of the benefits could be:
1   Return on the investment arising from the profits of the
    acquisition.
2   Additional overhead recovery at the home factories
    from increased sales.
3   Better understanding of the market, leading to easier
    penetration of other adjacent markets.
4   Opportunity to meet potential competitors on their own
    ground, so as to sharpen the company's product develop-
    ment approach.
The first benefit can be assessed reasonably accurately, the
second one less so, and the other two hardly at all. So if the
investment decision is taken in isolation it may be based
entirely on the return on investment and the other factors
ignored.

If, however, the decision is made as part of a strategic
plan, it may well be entirely satisfactory to accept a marginal
financial return in order to make progress in the other fields.
No investment is good or bad in isolation; it is only suitable
or otherwise as one stage in a plan.

Divestment decisions should follow much the same pattern.
It may be right to dispose of very profitable units if they do
not fit the long-term strategy, or because funds are needed to
further that strategy. It is *usually* right to close or dispose of
persistent loss-makers, but not always so. It depends on where
the company intends to go, and how it intends to get there.

Summary

The strategic plan is the instrument with which the chief

31

executive ensures that his overall view of the development of his business is transmitted to all the executives of the company, and is translated into detailed action programmes that will ensure the achievement of the business objectives. Within the strategic plan each executive is working to outline objectives for his own department. Because the strategic plan makes clear his objectives, opportunities and constraints, it defines the boundaries of his responsibility, but within those boundaries he can have considerable freedom of action. This freedom for executives to use their own initiative to contribute creatively to the development of the business is only possible if a strategic plan exists. If one does not exist, then the only way the chief executive can influence the course of the business is to direct the individual actions and decisions of his subordinates, which will stultify their initiative and limit their commitment. With a strategic plan, the chief executive has no need to interfere with specific day-to-day decisions or actions. He is not concerned with them, unless they represent major departures from the plan; he is just measuring achievement against the targets set. He is then increasing his own freedom and, paradoxically perhaps, his ability to check on, and monitor, the performance of his subordinates. Not only will he find more time to watch over the business, but also to think and to plan his next strategic plan, and to build and develop the team which alone will transform the plan into achievement.

3 Operational Planning

The need for a strategic plan was discussed in the previous chapter where it was made clear that the chief executive must be directly responsible for such a plan. But the achievement of objectives depends on concerted action in many different departments and, however well the plan has been communicated, only by the coordination of these activities will the expected results be achieved. A sound operational planning process is essential to convert the intentions of the strategic plan into a programme of action.

It could be argued that operational planning is the essence of any manager's job, that he is continually making long- and short-term plans and implementing them. To advocate an operational planning process seems akin to the 'motherhood is good' school of thinking, and invites the response 'so what else is new?'. There is something in this view; any kind of management process entails making a plan and seeing that it is carried out. The truth is, however, that in many companies most of such plans are of an *ad hoc* nature. They are made in response to events or problems arising, rather than from the intention of meeting the company's strategic objectives. They are essentially defensive actions rather than actions designed to further the company's development.

Defensive planning

Where this is true, and planning is largely concentrated on
defensive activities, the organisation concerned has a tendency
to go on doing what it is currently doing, but with steadily
deteriorating efficiency. The evidence for this is all around
us. Any bureaucracy will do as an example. A bureaucracy
is bound by rules that were originally intended to establish
an efficient service and to protect the users of the service
from arbitrary decisions by the bureaucrats. In practice, what
usually happens is that the service soon deteriorates and the
rules, far from defending the public from the bureaucrats,
operate in the reverse direction. One way in which this often
reveals itself is in the appeals procedure — usually, there is
some form of appeal available which enables anyone dissatisfied with the bureaucrat's interpretation of the rules to
apply to have his case reconsidered. In practice, the time
taken to adjudicate on an appeal is often so long that most
people will accept the rough injustice of the situation rather
than suffer a further delay.

There are many reasons why the effectiveness of an
organisation steadily deteriorates unless there is positive
planning. One such reason can be categorised as negative
improvement. An executive anxious to improve the system
makes changes which seem to be reasonable from his point
of view, but which have adverse effects in other parts of
the organisation that he does not foresee or take account of.

I remember working with a manufacturing executive who
was worried because his department had large adverse cost
variances and he was concerned to put this right. He
analysed the cost of each individual item manufactured
by his department and compared the cost with quotations
obtained from outside the company. He found that in many
cases he could buy the necessary parts more cheaply than he
could manufacture them. He came to the conclusion that
the problem arose because his facilities were not suitable for
the manufacture of some of the items, and decided that it
would be better to place that work with sub-contractors. He
was confident that he had solved his problem and sat back
and awaited the improved results. He felt that he had done

everything that a good executive should in the circumstances. He had identified the problem, examined the facts, isolated the cause and planned and implemented remedial steps. He was very upset when he found that his departmental variances worsened sharply during the succeeding months. As a good engineer he was quite hurt when the accountants pointed out to him that such a result was inevitable unless he was able to reduce his fixed costs in proportion to the amount of work subcontracted.

I am not telling this anecdote to illustrate the financial naivety of many otherwise competent managers but to make the point that, with an effective set of company operational plans, it would be difficult for such a circumstance to arise.

Another frequent cause of deteriorating performance is anxiety to achieve a single-valued objective. As an example, very few chief executives would instruct their heads of manufacturing to go for output at all costs, yet very often that is what the latter will in practice be doing. Output is monitored very closely by top management because it is directly linked with invoiced sales. The head of manufacturing knows that if output falls short of budget in any period invoiced sales will be low and he will be called to account. In such a situation he may well take extraordinary measures to achieve the required output. Excessive overtime may be worked, subcontractors may be asked to carry out work at very short notice without proper price negotiations, unsuitable processes may be used to try to avoid bottlenecks, quality standards may be reduced. The result of such actions may be that costs are pushed above the optimum level to such an extent that the profit and cash flow objectives of the company would have been much better served if a lower volume, more efficiently produced, had been accepted.

Many companies work as if they had single-valued objectives. Sales departments frequently treat sales volume as being of overriding importance. Where a sales department has this attitude and where prices or discounts are set by negotiation rather than by a predetermined price list, sales volume is often achieved at the expense of margin.

Few companies actually intend to set themselves single-valued objectives; they arise because of the absence of a plan and because the company is reacting to immediate pressures. Perhaps cash gets short, so there is a strong drive to optimise value of output, to reduce stocks, and get cash in from debtors. A few months later production costs climb sharply because stocks are now inadequate to sustain the required production level and the production programme is constantly being adjusted to make use of the materials that are available.

Positive planning

For these and very many other reasons of a similar nature a planning and control process is necessary not only to improve the performance of a business but also to prevent it from deteriorating.

One reason for an operational planning process is, therefore, to prevent the deterioration that will arise in any organisation if no positive planning system exists. The plans are required to maintain and to enhance the effectiveness of the business in carrying out its existing role. Arising from the plan, standards of performance will be established in every field of activity to enable adverse trends to be detected and remedied before they have a serious effect on the business as a whole.

The other main reason for an operational planning system is to be able to take the action necessary to achieve the objectives of the strategic plan. That is why the chief executive must be so very closely involved. Anything that changes the way the company carries out its business (even with the intention of improving its performance) has elements of risk that may not be obvious to those initiating the change. It is the chief executive's responsibility to monitor such decisions. This is true whatever the nature of the change. He cannot help being involved with major changes but without a company plan he may well not be aware of changes originally considered by other executives as being of lesser importance until they have started to have a baleful effect on the company's performance. Perhaps no decision is wholly irreversible, but some seemingly minor decisions can have far-reaching consequences and may be very difficult to reverse.

It is not suggested that the chief executive is the only person in a business who is allowed to initiate change. Far from it. But it is essential that changes are planned in advance and that the chief executive reviews the plans before they are implemented. In this way he knows what is going on and has time to intervene if he wishes to do so.

One purpose of a corporate planning system is, therefore, to ensure that changes are considered in advance and recorded and are formally approved by the chief executive. The corollory is that any changes not included in the operational plans are not allowed to be implemented without the chief executive's direct approval.

Responsibility for changes

This requirement is not intended to stifle initiative. No company can be really successful unless new ideas are generated at all levels. But any chief executive who wants to sleep easily at night needs to know what changes of practice are being initiated and to be in a position to halt or modify those that he considers undesirable. The existence of such a planning system gives the other executives freedom to take relevant actions to implement their plans without further reference to the chief executive. It is only in the absence of a plan that each and every step would have to be cleared with the chief executive, which can be a very time-consuming and frustrating process.

I do mean *all* except the most trivial changes should be included in the plan and be approved by the chief executive. It is surprising the extent to which relatively unimportant changes can have a profound effect upon business performance.

During my early career as a management consultant I was often called upon to make recommendations about failed productivity incentive schemes. Most of the schemes had been soundly established. What had gone wrong was that someone had introduced changes under the impression that they were fair and relatively trivial.

One example is the type of payment made for time the operatives are waiting for work or held up for any other

reason. Usually, when the scheme is set up, they are paid a
fixed proportion of their basic rate for lost time, but soon
there comes pressure to be paid average bonus for such
periods, because the delay 'is not their fault'. If the point is
conceded labour costs rapidly escalate. The reason is simple
The change, so harmless in itself, has created a powerful
incentive to maximise the *booking* of waiting time. It
reduces the number of hours booked to productive work and
artificially increases the rate at which bonus can be earned.

I have known companies whose profitability was virtually
eliminated because of the excess labour costs arising from
apparently innocuous amendments of this kind to schemes
which were originally implemented to have precisely the
reverse effect. I repeat, therefore, that a chief executive
should be aware of all changes of this nature before they
are introduced.

Do I really expect the chief executive of General Motors
to know all the changes going on in his vast empire? No, of
course not, but one of the reasons why large organisations
have to be broken down into smaller units is to enable the
chief executives of these units to be in a position to be
properly informed. My definition of a chief executive is
one who is responsible for a substantially autonomous unit,
the performance of which is subject to normal market forces.

It follows that within a major group there are likely to be
layers of chief executives at divisional and company level and,
provided that they are operating generally at arm's length
from other members of the group, the definition holds.

In such circumstances, what is a matter of unimportant
detail to the group chief executive may be a crucial factor
in the plan of the manager in charge of one of the subsidiary
companies. It is up to the chief executives at each level to
decide the nature of changes that must be planned or
individually approved, and to make sure that their intentions
in this respect are followed.

Resistance to planning

It can be very difficult to introduce operational planning into

a company that has not practised it before. There may be a
great reluctance to commit plans to paper. I have often
heard executives say that although planning may work elsewhere, they have distinct problems that do not permit making
reliable enough forecasts for preparation of such detailed
plans.

The resistance to planning may come from a confused idea
of what is meant by 'accuracy' in forecasting. All that may
be necessary is to convince the objectors that a forecast need
only be as accurate as is necessary for the purpose in hand.
Quite often it may be found that an executive has a very good
feeling for the upper and lower limits expected for any given
factor. He just finds it difficult to decide on a single figure
or is concerned that, if he quotes it, he may later find himself impaled upon it.

There are more ways and means of getting nearer to the
truth than are apparent at first glance. This is not the place
to go into the various forecasting techniques available, but
one way to overcome resistance to this aspect of planning
is to expose the executives concerned to such techniques
by means of training courses.

Planners and executors

If there is a separate planning department it needs to do its
work in cooperation with the various operating departments,
otherwise the plan is quite likely to be disregarded. As an
illustration of this I well remember an occasion when I was
talking to one of the managers of the largest German subsidiary of a well known international group. He was in an
expansive mood that day, and the conversation had long
left the subject I had come to discuss. The manager was
ruminating about his past career, his present position and
his lost ambitions. It was when this led him to talk about
his relationship with head office that the tone changed and
a suggestion of bitterness crept in. Suddenly, he opened the
bottom drawer of his desk and brought out a computer
printout, which was about 10 cm thick.

'My dear sir, do you know what this is? This is my

monthly programme. I get it during the last week of the previous month and as you can see, it is all beautifully set out. Do you know what I do with it? This!', and he dropped the printout back into the drawer. 'But how do you explain to head office any discrepancies between your production and the programme?', he laughed. 'I have exaggerated a bit. I know which six or seven items really count. I have a quick look and then it goes in there. You see, they cannot possibly be right in their forecasts of requirements of all the various items and types of pack, considering the number of factories we have, with the ups and downs of production and the changes in demand for the product. And then they could never investigate more than a fraction of the variances anyhow. But I know broadly what can and should be produced without all this.' 'Why then, do you think, they send it to you?' 'God alone knows, I doubt whether *they* do!'

This is not an unusual attitude where planning is separated from operations and where it is perhaps being carried out in too fine a detail for the functional level concerned. Operational planning belongs with operations — only strategic planning can be confined to head office.

Features of the operational plan

Any worthwhile operational plan has five main features:
1   A restatement of the company's strategic plan and objectives as far as they relate to the planning period.
2   A statement of the assumptions about external and internal influences on which the plan is based.
3   A descriptive account of the company's intended actions to achieve the objectives defined in the strategic plan within the constraints arising from the statement of assumptions.
4   A summary of the key events necessary to achieve the plan.
5   A quantitative plan (sales volume, costs, productivity, capital investment, cash flow, etc.).

Restatement of the strategic plan

A restatement of the company's strategic plan may seem an unnecessary exercise if everyone concerned already has a copy, but it is surprising how often one finds that a company's operational plans bear no relationship to its stated long-term objectives.

What often happens is that when an exciting opportunity presents itself, the possibility of exploiting it is discussed and, almost without anyone actually deciding to do so, the possibility hardens into an intention to do so. The opportunity itself may be splendid, but it may be quite wrong for that particular company at that particular time. Indeed the diversion of attention that it entails may well prevent the achievement of much more important aims.

A common focus for such diversionary activities is new product development. There is always another slot in the market that a company could fill if it had a mind to do so. If there is any tendency towards sales domination, it may seek to fill that slot regardless of whether the decision accords with long-term development intentions.

To use a military analogy, it is rather like an expeditionary force besieging all the wealthy towns that lie on its path, rather than going all-out to capture the strategic pass which is the key to the whole province.

Still, for most companies, unexpected opportunities arise from time to time. There may be a chance to acquire another business, or some additional premises, perhaps adjacent to existing plant; or a competitor withdraws from a market leaving his main agent open to offers and perhaps short of cash.

What does the chief executive do? Does he say: 'This is not part of my strategic plan and, therefore, I will not divert my resources to it'. Or does he say: 'This is a chance which will not come my way again. I'll take the opportunity.'

There is no general answer to this, except that the plan must be an important factor in the considerations. An unplanned opportunity which offers a different path to the same general objectives would obviously merit very close examination. One that tends to take the company in a new

41

direction would have to be very attractive indeed to justify close consideration because it would entail rewriting the strategic plan with the consequent effects on every other part of the business. If the original plan has been well conceived it would be important to be very sure that the change was a real improvement and not just a case of the grass being greener elsewhere.

There was one company which planned to build up its export trade and came to the view that it should set up its own sales force in the biggest of its overseas markets. However, just when the plan was completed the news came that one of its main agents in another territory was for sale. The funds intended to establish the new venture were immediately diverted to this purchase so as not to miss the opportunity. However, the effect of the change was that, just because an opportunity had arisen to reduce the time scale of growth by buying an established business, the company virtually abandoned a carefully selected market for one considerably less attractive. In effect it traded long-term growth for a short-term advantage.

This is typical of cases in which a good opportunity diverts a company from its declared aims — the short-term result may be good, but the company is not fundamentally improved by it.

So product development is not the only field in which *ad hoc* departures from strategy are to be found. In many other areas — such as the entry into new markets, investment in new plant and facilities, and the acquisition of other businesses — it is necessary to ensure that policy objectives are observed.

I am not, of course, saying that new opportunities should always be ignored unless they are in line with the company's stated strategy; once in a while an opportunity comes up which is so good that it justifies a complete review of strategy. I am saying, however, that it should be developed only on that basis, otherwise it should be ignored. A restatement of those aims in the operational plans helps to make sure that that is so.

Statement of assumptions

Paradoxically, once executives have accepted that the system is of benefit to them, they go to the opposite extreme and quantify elements in the plan without thinking through and recording the basic assumptions on which the figures are based. If this happens, then the assumptions which were in everyone's mind when the figures were agreed may be long forgotten when the forecasts are tested by reality. This is harmful because quite often the forecasts are conditional. Someone says: 'What would happen if we did . . . ?' Figures are worked out and then become incorporated in the plan without the underlying conditions having been stated. Any figures written in the plan gain their own authority totally unrelated to the reliability of the evidence on which they were based.

The remedy is clear. In any planning process, first clarify the basic assumptions on which the plan will be based and record them. Only then can the numerical aspects of the plan be given.

It is also important to write down the assumptions upon which any plan is based, because they are frequently forgotten later when actual performance is being compared with the plan. In deciding the reason for any shortfall in performance, it can be very useful to know whether the execution of the plan has been inadequate, or whether the assumptions on which it was based have proved to be inaccurate. In this context, the assumptions are essentially concerned with events and trends which are outside the control of management. Typically these include:

1   General economic trends   It is usually necessary to take account of general economic trends in forecasting a company's sales turnover. The importance of this will vary from one company to another. If a company is breaking into a new market and has a very small share of that market it may consider itself little affected by the overall trend, because its intended growth is at the expense of already established competitors. On the other hand, when a company has market dominance the general economic trends in the market in which it operates may be of fundamental importance in determining the sales levels to be expected.

2   Rates of inflation   Inflation has a most important bearing on the amount of cash the company will require to sustain a given real output. At times of high inflation, cash flow may be a more important restraint on growth than the availability of orders. If this is so, then it is important to have a pricing policy which ensures that the orders that can be filled generate high profit margins.

The rate of inflation will also decide how 'real' any profits are. If the company is operating an inflation accounting system then presumably financial planning will be done on the same basis, but if not, taking a general view on inflation will indicate the need to generate higher profit to make sure that the net worth of the company increases at a higher rate than inflation itself.

3   Specific market trends   Apart from the general economic trends referred to in the previous paragraph, there will be assumptions about specific changes in the company's own market. There are leads and lags in any economic situation so that the economic peaks for individual markets will arise at different times during the economic cycle. Superimposed on the general economic and market trends is a long-term rise and decay of particular market requirements.

A company making hi-fi equipment, for example, would need to make assumptions about the general economic conditions in its market and the disposable income levels available, the share of these disposable incomes that will be devoted to the acquisition of hi-fi equipment, the spread of expenditure in various hi-fi product groupings and the share the company itself can hope to capture.

4   Technological trends   These trends are leading every product towards obsolescence (although at varying speeds). Sometimes the trends are obvious, as in the case of slide rules in competition with cheap electronic calculators or the effect of glass-reinforced plastic on more traditional materials, such as timber or fabricated metal. Such technological developments are arising continually. The problem is to identify them in time and to judge how fast they are becoming reality.

Failure to adjust brings penalties. I once met a labourer in a factory mass-producing cheap furniture. He was an energetic man in his late 50s, and his attitude to his work and his obviously active mind made him seem out of place doing an unskilled job. In an expansive mood one day, he told me how he came to be there: 'I had a nice little business of my own, building pleasure boats. You know, the sort of boat you hire by the hour in a local park. I had up to 20 men working for me and I was doing very well. Then, suddenly, it went, almost overnight. It was not a limited company, so I had to sell up everything, even my home.' 'What went wrong?', I asked. 'Well, you see, I was building in wood. My men were crafts-men in wood. I did not know anything about glass fibre or plastic, and when I heard about them, I thought they would never catch on. But it killed my business.'

Today we may think that the transition from wood to glass fibre, which turned this small businessman into a labourer, was predictable. But right now, carbon fibre is at the stage that glass fibre reached 20 years ago, and it may challenge other materials in unthought-of applications that one day will seem equally obvious.

Apart from direct competition, new discoveries can have other far-reaching effects on industry. 'Safe' food additives suddenly come under suspicion of causing cancer and are banned. Aerosol propellants are claimed to be threatening the world's ecological stability. Even popular brands of baby food are suddenly found to be potentially lethal. Change can be abrupt and can threaten one's very livelihood.

There are many other external factors such as probable interest rates, manpower availability, government policy changes. It is not possible to write down assumptions about every external factor, but at least there should be an attempt to identify those external trends that have the biggest effect on the company's business and get information about them on paper.

Descriptive plan

The descriptive plan is the link between the objectives and requirements of the strategic plan, the assumptions, and the quantitative plan which will follow.

It seems best to treat this as a simple narrative, as if describing to an uninvolved third party what the company intends to do during the planning period, the changes that will be achieved, and the dates at which they will come into effect.

Key events

From the above narrative the key events can be identified and tabulated. These act as useful checkpoints when performance is being monitored. Also these events will include such changes as price increases, launch of new products, commissioning of new plant, etc., to which the quantative plan can be anchored.

Normally this will consist of all those items which are required for effective budgetary control such as:

1   Sales forecast.
2   Production plan.
3   Cost budgets for each department.
4   Capital investment budget.
5   Profit plan.
6   Cash flow forecast.

Responsibility for planning

The basic rule is that whoever is responsible for implementing the plan must be involved in its preparation. This means that every head of department prepares a plan for his department. In most companies, the sales department plan has to come first, because the sales forecast is the crucial factor which determines the income available to operate the company. When the sales forecast is known then most other departmental plans can move forward in parallel.

The chief executive would normally review the assumptions and requirements of the strategic plan and examine the main departmental plans. As soon as the summary is available he would decide whether the envisaged outcome is acceptable. Usually he will find that changes will be necessary. The process is again essentially a reiterative one with several stages of review and refinement before an outcome is developed that is regarded as satisfactory by the chief executive.

Most plans are constructed at a number of levels, so that the plans at operating level contain the fine detail and, as they are combined to build the plan at the next level, much of the detail is shed, until, at the highest level, the plans deal only in the most important parameters.

Method of planning

There are essentially two ways of arriving at a quantitative plan for any department. The first is to examine what has taken place in the previous planning period, adjust for any changes that are anticipated in the level of activity in that department, and prepare a new plan directly from this. The other, which is referred to as zero-base budgeting, is to build up the plan from first principles.

To illustrate the two methods, consider a manufacturing department which is attempting to forecast expenditure on small tools for the next budget year. The first method will be to examine expenditure for the current year, review the figures with the executives concerned and adjust for any changes in levels of activity anticipated in the coming year, adjust for the effects of inflation and adjust for any plans to use the existing tools more effectively. The resultant figure becomes the budget for the following year.

The zero-base budget for the same department would be obtained by considering each activity of the department, separately assessing all the operations that require small tools, assessing tool life and the frequency of replacement and estimating the replacement cost for each category of tools; and so, step-by-step, building up a budget from first principles.

Of the two methods the first is reasonably reliable in

predicting what will actually happen in the budget period but it can easily conceal a long-term lack of control and excess expenditure. Zero-base budgets are much more laborious to produce and perhaps less likely to be accurate because a big range of judgements is necessary in setting them up; but they are more likely to reveal any areas of inefficiency.

In practice a company which bases all its plans on previous performance is likely to show a deteriorating situation, because any inefficiencies in one period become built into the plan for the following one. To do all budgets from the zero-base can be very time-consuming. What is best is a combination of the two systems, with most items being planned on a prior-year basis and a few selected ones on a zero-base system.

Summary

The chief executive's part in planning is to ensure that:
1   There is a planning process.
2   The plans are the result of the best judgements that can be made at the time.
3   The plans are directed towards the company's strategic objectives.
4   Any changes planned in the way the company does business have the chief executive's personal approval.
5   The planned profit level is adequate and that a satisfactory cash flow will be generated.

The only way the chief executive can avoid becoming immersed in the day-to-day activities of business to such an extent that he has no time for anything else is for him to devote enough time once a year to make sure that there is a comprehensive plan. If he does this, and if he makes sure that the plan is sufficiently detailed and supported by an adequate control system, then, by monitoring results against the plan, he can maintain control of the business and need only get involved in detail when there are significant departures from the plan. A good planning system, therefore, allows the chief executive to concentrate on major issues and on the long-term future of his company without wondering all the time whether all is going well in eavery department and in every aspect of the business.

48

4 Control

In many small companies the chief executive exercises control
by being personally involved in everything that is going on.
There is nothing wrong with that; it works very well while a
company is small but the trouble is that some companies
persist too long with this form of control. The chief executive
then ceases to be able to know what is taking place and he
makes decisions based on inadequate information. If this is
allowed to happen the company's performance will eventually
decline.

Habits and behaviour that were admirable in the formative
days of a business, that may indeed have been responsible for
its success, become a drag and may do damage once the
company has grown too large for the 'personal' mode of
control.

I remember once meeting the chief executive and co-
founder of a successful small company who brushed aside the
need for 'paper' to control his business. 'The best control
there is', he told me, 'is when I, the boss, walk into my factory
at 8 a.m. and stand in the middle of the workshop watching
what is going on.' There is much to be said for this point of
view. But when the business grows, there comes a time when
'the boss' is able to see only a fraction of 'what is going on',

with the result that any corrective action will be taken far too late.

The alternative is, of course, control by comparison against plans and budgets, and for the chief executive to take personal action only in the case of a significant departure from targets set.

There is little purpose in having plans without a system of controls that will ensure their implementation. The only certainty about them is that they will be wrong, or at least the outcome will not be as planned unless corrective actions are taken throughout their currency.

Assumptions will be wrong. One has only to read the financial press and compare the different economic forecasts prepared by bodies of repute to know that no-one can really be sure of the future rate of economic change even if all are agreed on the main direction of that change.

Market trends are also notoriously difficult to forecast when a product is relatively new. It is fairly easy to assess the market for the *existing* use of an *existing* product, but it is very hard indeed to get an accurate assessment of the demand arising from a *new* application and harder still if both the product and the application are new.

Competitors are very unpredictable too. They will keep on innovating just when one's own market strategy has discounted such a possibility. Even more irritating is the fact that although many of their innovations will not prove successful, it is very hard to know which, and very tempting to attempt to smother all of them with a matched response. There will also be product replacement from enterprises that were considered in no way competitive.

'Controllable' costs will not in the event prove to be as controllable as anticipated, and some will fall outside the budget limits.

Every assumption in a plan will prove, to some extent, to be wrong. The only saving grace will be that with any luck, and with reasonable care during the budgeting process, the balance between favourable and unfavourable variations will prove to be a fairly equal one.

One of the biggest weaknesses in planning is over-optimism. Murphy's first law says that if things can go wrong they will, and as they always can they always will. But in most plans not enough allowance is made for things going wrong. For instance, the time taken to design and develop a new product, to carry out prototype testing, to organise and implement a programme of field trials, and then to tool-up and get the product in volume to the eventual customers is very often grossly under-estimated.

Obtaining and commissioning new plant is another field in which over-optimism is prevalent. The difficulty here is that it is too often assumed that plant will be fully commissioned shortly after it has been delivered, whereas in practice it may take a considerable time to plan and provide the ancillary tooling, to train operatives and to overcome the teething troubles that accompany any change.

There will also be plain errors in implementation, in any business that is moving forward rapidly most executives are under pressure. The majority of their decisions are based on previous experience rather than detailed analysis. This must be true because in most real-life business situations constantly changing events leave little time for adequate research before decisions are taken. This means that some of them will be wrong — however good the executives.

There is, therefore, a pattern of constant deviation from plans in every degree and in every facet. A control system is essential to quantify significant deviations, identify those which are important, and give some indication of the kind of remedial action necessary.

Control against plans

Control must always be by comparison with a plan. There are many companies which circulate a considerable amount of information on such things as rate of order intake, production volume, invoiced sales, stock and debtor levels, profitability, etc., without the support of an operational plan. The difficulty in such a situation is that, without a great deal of additional work, it is almost impossible to know whether the results presented are satisfactory or not (except perhaps the net profit figure or the net cash flow).

If the control is against a plan the executive concerned needs only to scan the variances to know what needs to be done. If the same figures are presented on their own, it is much more difficult to know exactly what has gone wrong. As an example, a big jump in the value of stocks in a given accounting period may be an indication of poor inventory management; but it may be because a plan to increase sales needs a stock build-up before the actual launch. In a single-product business such a reason would be obvious, but when there is an extensive product range, with varying margins, and possibly a mixture of manufactured and factored products, it may be quite difficult to assign causes. If there is a plan then it is easy to see whether the cause of the growth in stock was intended or not, and furthermore it will be known whether it has been taken into account in the company's cash flow projection.

The first level of control is, therefore, comparison with plan, usually on a weekly or monthly basis. The question of what should be controlled varies enormously from one company to another. Obviously, it will include such factors as order intake, productivity of labour, of plant and processes, of capital, total output in volume and financial terms, cost data and cash flow.

The chief executive will not want to see it all; far from it. Each executive will get the information relevant to his own department and the chief executive will get a summary of the key figures and reports of any major departures from plan.

As such control information takes some time to prepare, I have often found it useful to identify the really crucial factors and get the figures for these within a few days of the end of the accounting period. What is crucial depends on the business. It may be unit sales, gross turnover, capacity utilised, or any one of a whole range of other possibilities. Once the factor or factors have been correctly identified, it is surprising how easy it is to predict the result for the period with a good standard of accuracy.

One useful exercise is for the chief executive to say to himself: 'If I were in Outer Mongolia and could only know 10 facts about my business each month, which 10 would I choose?'. Whatever the choice, they are the ones to watch in normal times.

As a general rule, I would say that attention to cash flow is more important than attention to profit. I have seen many profitable companies in deep trouble because the cash flow was not adequately controlled. In the long term, control of cash flow ensures both profitability and survival. Control of profit alone may not do so.

Control data of the type described above will take care of the current performance of the business but will not safeguard the future. It is necessary to establish similar control procedures concerning that part of the plan which deals with development projects. The form of such a plan will vary from a few key dates to a complete planning network depending on the complexity of the project. The chief executive needs to monitor the most important of the key dates and the cost of the various development stages.

I have found that this is best done by holding regular formal review discussions with the heads of the departments concerned. The meetings should be formal and should be as small as possible — just the chief executive and the manager concerned, only calling in other managers if their presence is necessary to discuss a particular topic to which they can contribute. Notes of the meeting should be issued in the form of progress statements and forecasts of future progress.

Typically, therefore, I would envisage a chief executive holding progress discussions with each of his four or five senior managers at least once a month to review the progress of their individual departments, and holding one general management meeting, with them all present, to coordinate activities where they interact. As I have indicated elsewhere, if the management team is working well together, informal discussions will be taking place on a continuous basis and the formal meetings should exist largely to confirm understandings already arrived at, and to make sure that nothing has been missed.

Control over people

The availability of a control system based on comparison with plans and budgets makes it possible to monitor the performance of executives in an objective way. Each of them has agreed to a certain set of targets for his department, and the degree to which the targets have been achieved is generally a matter of fact, not of opinion. Such comparisons are useful just because they are objective. However, they are not the whole answer. Even if the targets have been missed by a wide margin there may be special circumstances, but obviously the achievement of self-imposed objectives is a very powerful motivating force. There is some danger in attempting to assess an executive entirely on the performance of his own department; he may then tend to optimise its performance to the disadvantage of the company as a whole. Apart from the direct effect of this on the company's performance, it may also lead to the executive being regarded as a bad colleague and break up the unity of the management team.

The man himself may be keen to make an impact and to enhance his reputation. He therefore goes for the short-term solution, which may be injurious in the long run, or have an unfavourable effect on other parts of the business. Sometimes this is done quite consciously.

'I do not give a damn. I know I used to preach to the board that we must ensure that our salesmen sell a product mix that accords with our production capacities. But now . . . . ' This was an acquaintance of mine, a man with a reputation for versatility and for being a go-getter. He had been asked to 'hold the fort' temporarily while the sales department was without a head. 'But now', he continued, 'I shall get the sales by hook or by crook, and the production boys better make sure that they can deliver!'

It is not usually as blatant as that, but the tendency is there and must be guarded against.

It follows that a chief executive who bases his judgements about the performance of his subordinates on the achievement of their department against plans will have an essential input to his assessment, but will be less than adequately informed about the contribution of each individual to the overall company performance; there is a need to seek information of a more general nature.

In another context also, periodic control data is inadequate to give a chief executive all the information he needs because he is interested not only in the facts but in their causes. The fact that, for instance, sales are lower than in the same period last year, is an important piece of data; the fact that his biggest customer has started to stock a competitor's product is equally, or more, important. A person might pick up the change in buying habits but a computer, for instance, will probably not have been programmed to do so and will never say: 'I wonder why . . . . ? '

A chief executive needs an input of gossip, speculation and hearsay as well as of hard data; it is the former which can give him clues to the understanding of some of the data and — even more important — may provide the first early warning of a change in trends. Comprehensive management information systems, however desirable for other reasons, may not give him this, and may preoccupy him to such an extent that he has no time to get it elsewhere.

That means getting around the business, meeting important customers or suppliers; all the things a busy chief executive finds so hard to allocate time for. Even in the case of an industrial organisation where all departments are on one site, the chief executive may be so busy that he very rarely goes around the factory or through the design laboratories. I have known situations in relatively small companies where the chief executive's presence in the factory was an annual event preceded by much cleaning up and painting of white lines. When the day came the great man and his entourage whisked through the factory, seeing only what it had been decided to show him, meeting only those people steered his way, so that neither the chief executive nor the other employees benefitted by the visit, except to ensure that the factory was tidy at least once a year.

That is not for me. I believe that regular informal visits are essential. They should be as frequent as is possible within the physical constraints of the distances to be covered and the sites to be examined.

On such visits the chief executive should have a general

walk round the site and choose one particular aspect to examine in greater depth without too much warning about what he has in mind. Typically, he may look at such matters as control of product quality or inventory management or treatment of customer complaints. It does not matter too much what he decides to examine, but the fact that it is known that he does do so from time to time itself helps to ensure that slackness does not creep into the organisation.

In this context examination means *in depth*. In the example of looking into the treatment of customer complaints, it would start by reading some of the original letters selected at random, studying the replies, checking the delay between complaint and response and assessing the customer's final satisfaction or otherwise. Of course, these are trivial details with which the chief executive should not usually have to concern himself. But he is not really investigating the details of the complaints, only making sure that they are effectively and systematically dealt with, which is quite a different matter.

The other need in such a visit is to discuss with the executives on site, informally, their views about the present state of their business, their own plans and aspirations, and to understand how they see the strengths and weaknesses of the organisation.

Where problems are known to exist he needs to get their views on the causes and how they can be put right. Often these may be quite at odds with the head office view and, except where self-preservation is involved, are as likely to be right. Where there are contentious issues and certain steps have been taken he must understand fully the reasons for taking such steps.

He must flout the rule which says that it is unwise for a chief executive to get too deeply immersed in the petty details of a problem. It is a great temptation to use this very sound rule to brush aside a problem and to leave it to the man on the spot. But in pressing for total clarity he may well find that the reason for many an action lies in the confusion of thought of that man. By clarifying his own mind he thus clarifies also the minds of his subordinates.

Often people will baffle him with jargon. They may not do

this consciously. It may just indicate the way they think, but he has to cut through it, to know what they are driving at. Often he will discover that a woolly presentation conceals confusion of thought. If he does not quite understand a point and lets it go at that, he may never find this out and nothing will ever be done to clarify things.

All such visits and the ensuing discussions have a two-fold objective: the chief executive is going round the business to get a qualitative view about what is going on, to get to know his executives better and to find out how they work, how they think and feel about the business; but he is also there to communicate to the employees on the site his own ideas and attitudes and to indicate those things which he regards as important.

Remedial actions

What does the chief executive do if any of the controls indicate that something is wrong? As in most things there is quite a fine balance between not doing enough or doing too much. He must give the executives directly concerned an opportunity to put things right themselves. This may be very difficult if the right course of action is immediately clear to the chief executive and he feels that he could resolve the problem at a stroke. But only by not interfering too early and giving his subordinates a chance to do their own jobs will he find out how capable they are, and allow them to grow in stature and to learn to assume wider responsibilities.

Unless the problem is of momentous importance, his first step must be to bring it to the attention of the executives concerned and let them resolve it. He should take specific action himself only in two situations. The first, as indicated, is when the problem may have such far-reaching potential consequences that he connot afford not to take action at once. A severe product quality problem which is damaging the company's reputation might come into this category, or an impending cash crisis.

The other situation arises when the executives concerned

have had an opportunity to resolve the problem and have failed to do so. It is imperative then that the matter is not allowed to continue and that the chief executive takes decisive and effective action. When this arises I would accept the case for overkill. Executives must know that, although the chief executive is reluctant to interfere, he will use all the means at his disposal to ensure that problems are resolved.

I favour overkill in such a situation because I believe that every management problem is soluble, and that the main reason why they are not resolved by the executives directly responsible is that they become hidebound by the current attitudes and practices within the company and will not look widely enough for a solution. They allow small priorities to override larger ones, they reject uncomfortable solutions in the hope that something will turn up to avoid the necessity of taking hard action. They would rather accept the chronic worry of familiar problems than the acute demands of open-ended thought and drastic change. The chief executive must prove to them not only that substandard performance is unacceptable, but that it is not inevitable.

What is my evidence for such a contention? In many businesses a change of management brings a dramatic change in the fortunes of the business. When a new manager takes over, he examines everything without any pre-conceived notions, and then takes a few, often quite simple steps and transforms it. For instance, one business had a monopoly of its markets and yet was doing little better than break even and produce a totally unacceptable return on the capital invested in the business. Local management failed to resolve the situation and, in the end, it was sold by the group to which it belonged. The new owners just put the prices up and overnight the business was healthy. It sounds so obvious when it is written down, but the management were very concerned about offending their customers and were completely unaware of the strength of their own position. The new owners had done their homework before the acquisition and knew that the customers were locked into that particular product, because it was used in their own end-product and it would take at least two years to make changes. A price rise might cause a quick flurry of agitation but, provided it is accompanied by good service in every other respect, it will soon be forgotten, as it was in this particular business.

Local management is often blind to situations of this kind, and accepts such features as inflated overhead costs, unnecessarily large inventories, too narrow margins and excessive product proliferation, either because it has always been so as it lacks the will to change it, or perhaps most of all because it is not prepared to take the *risk* of doing so. The chief executive must change it and he is paid to take the risk.

The most important benefit an effective control system brings to the chief executive is peace of mind. He knows what is happening, knows what is going well and what is going badly. He knows the men involved, their quality, their aptitudes, their hopes and frustrations. He knows what they are trying to do to change the company, and he knows that the control system will give him the time and the knowledge to intervene, if and when it becomes necessary.

5 Team-building and Team-leading

Observation suggests that in the majority of cases it is the ability to select the right team that makes a chief executive successful.

This may seem to contradict the assertion made in Chapter 1 that the main distinguishing factor in a chief executive's job is his duty to take risks on behalf of his company. However, even the most autocratic chief executives (perhaps the autocratic ones more than most) are heavily dependent on the input they receive from every part of their organisation.

Every input is a mixture of fact and judgement. This is always true in business decisions because none of the important questions a businessman seeks to answer can have absolute answers.

In private life we constantly make decisions without testing or even querying the assumptions which led to them. One example is the behaviour of shoppers when confronted with a choice between several products, each of which will satisfy their particular need. Many will reject the cheapest on offer because 'at that price it can't be any good'. The unspoken assumption is 'you get what you pay for'. But in fact, consumer organisations have shown that one cannot take it for granted that there is a close correlation between quality and price. We rely on untested notions of this kind when making buying decisions because it is just not possible to become expert in all the fields in which a choice has to be made. We therefore choose on the basis of price or on such matters as country of origin, appearance and a host of other factors that may or may not have a bearing on the performance we are seeking.

Managers have much the same problems. They cannot test most of the premises on which they base their actions.

For instance, a fundamental question that a chief executive often has to consider is: 'If we develop a product with these characteristics, at this cost, what market share can we achieve with it?'. Any answer to that question involves judgements about customers' responses, upon actions currently being taken by competitors which may only be guessed at, and upon economic and technological trends which are notoriously difficult to forecast.

The chief executive cannot make all the judgements himself; the sheer mass of data is far too great for that. All he can do is to assemble the views of his specialist colleagues on the various factors, form his own judgement about their validity, consider the downside risk if they are wrong, and then make a decision. His decision is heavily influenced not just by the positive inputs of his subordinates, but also by what they choose to leave out.

There is also a vast gulf between decision and achievement. The quality of execution of any policy is entirely dependent on the executives who are carrying it out. Every plan ever made is imperfect. Some are better than others but even the very best need intelligent and flexible execution.

It follows that the competence of a chief executive can be judged by the quality of the team he has around him, and the ability of its members to work well together. If his immediate subordinates are able and resourceful men who are committed to the success of the business, they are likely to speak honestly and openly about any situation under discussion within the top management team. The chief executive will then be getting good advice, and the quality of his own decisions will be better than they would have been without such support.

If the chief executive surrounds himself with second-rate men, the quality of the advice that he is given is likely to be inadequate not just because of their limited intelligence and perception. The incumbents may indeed recognise their own inadequacy and be led to defend their own positions (perhaps unconsciously) by telling the chief executive what they think he wants to hear, rather than what they really believe.

A similar problem arises in the matter of execution of policy: inadequate subordinates are likely to feel insecure and threatened by able young men on their own staffs. The latter are then unlikely to be given much freedom of decision or action. This may be the result of a genuinely conservative attitude to the business; but more often it arises out of the recognition that a period of heightened change poses a special threat to those who have an inadequate grasp of their present jobs. Inadequate men, therefore, may suppress initiative on the part of their subordinates and take a narrow view of any policy decisions imposed from the top, interpreting them by the letter rather than by the spirit.

Another way in which inadequacy is exemplified is in a *laissez faire* attitude to actions of subordinates, so that personal rivalries will play an increasing part in determining the performance of the business.

If the quality of top management is inadequate this is, therefore, likely to have repercussions throughout the management structure. Any good men who are appointed will soon recognise the nature of their environment and seek more promising opportunities elsewhere, and a climate of mediocrity will become self-perpetuating.

At the other extreme, if the top team are of high calibre they will attract able men to work for them and, by their example and their demands, they will stretch and develop their subordinates, so that, progressively, the whole management team becomes a more effective instrument of policy.

The calibre of the whole management team is, therefore, decided at the very top, and this in turn will influence decisively its capacity for success or failure throughout the whole business.

Organisational structure

Team-building starts with consideration of the organisational structure and the chief executive must decide first on the most appropriate structure for the business before turning to questions of personalities.

The form of organisation is dependent upon the strategic plan. It seems to be common-sense to decide first what the company is going to do, and then the kind of organisation it needs to do it. But to put this particular piece of common-sense into practice is not always easy, and quite often the reverse happens — the existing form of structure strongly influences the strategic plan. This does not happen deliberately; executives unconsciously adopt policies appropriate to the existing form of organisation. For example, if a company is organised by product groups, it is very easy to assume that each division will continue as a separate entity and will, therefore, require its own future product range. It can be very hard for executives within such a structure to decide that one of the product groups has reached the end of its life cycle and should be phased out, whereas with another form of structure — a functional one for example — such a possibility might be much more readily apparent.

Still, as mentioned in the previous chapter, future strategy grows out of a company's past and, therefore, it is quite likely that an existing structure will be appropriate in the future. It is, however, necessary to make a conscious effort to disregard the structure when thinking about strategy, to make sure that the conditioning effect is not obscuring an attractive opportunity that might entail structural change.

In working out the strategic plan, a number of key areas will have been identified and objectives will have been set in relation to them. It is necessary to adopt an organisational structure which will ensure concentration on the achievement of these objectives. The boundaries of the responsibilities of each major subdivision of the company should be set in such a way as to give maximum freedom of judgement and decision-taking to the senior executives responsible for achieving the objectives. Of course, no department within a larger company can be truly autonomous; but the greater

63

the degree of autonomy within the structure, and the closer the objectives of the semi-autonomous units so created match the identified objectives of the business, the easier it is for the chief executive to motivate his team.

The dependence of structure on business strategy makes the former a dynamic concept, with the consequence that regular reviews of structure become necessary as the policies of the business develop and change. It is a view of business based on an organic model rather than a mechanistic one which in turn will ultimately determine one's attitude toward centralisation and decentralisation.

Decentralise

There are many differing views about the relative advantages of centralised versus decentralised organisations. Certainly no business can be entirely one or the other, and both attitudes to organisation have proved successful in a variety of business situations. My personal preference is to decentralise, and to delegate authority and responsibility as far down the management chain as can be achieved without obvious duplication of resources, and without sacrificing the benefits of scale where these have a bearing upon business effectiveness. This approach involves more people looking for opportunities, resolving problems and generally using their initiative to achieve the objectives of the business than would be the case with a centralised organisational pattern. It is also the only way I know to develop younger managers, and to separate the able from the merely convincing. It carries the penalty that executives must be allowed to make mistakes, and the chief executive must restrain his natural desire to intervene even when he thinks that a mistake is being made. If he is proven right, the executive concerned will have gained a new insight, if he is proven wrong the chief executive himself will have learnt something new.

For the chief executive knowingly to let mistakes happen may seem to be an abdication of his responsibility. But the cost of the mistake must be set against all the successful decisions and judgements by the same executive, and it is not possible to have one without the other.

In a centralised organisation, the major decisions will be those of the chief executive, the other executives mainly doing what they are told. If the chief executive is exceptionally able, the proportion of correct decisions may be high for quite some time. But as his subordinates become aware of the fact that all key decisions are being taken out of their hands, the good ones will leave and the less capable will be happy to transfer more responsibility for decision-making to him. As the chief executive drives away those of his subordinates who are prepared to use their own initiative, he will be forced to take an even greater proportion of decisions himself. The pressure on his time will prevent him from adequately examining the issues affected by his decisions. He will become engaged in an endless bout of instant decision-making and the quality of his decisions will accordingly decline.

All chief executives are under a temptation to interfere with the decisions of their subordinates, particularly in the fields in which they have a professional expertise. Occasionally, if a matter is of outstanding importance, it is the chief executives responsibility to intervene; otherwise it is in the chief executive's own interest to resist the temptation.

All structures are imperfect

There is one other important thing to be said about organisational structure that may appear to contradict some of the earlier comments: there is nothing more tempting, when business problems arise, than to tinker with the organisational structure in the hope that this will bring an improvement. Some businesses are perpetually in a turmoil of reorganisation and it is a common management consultant's ploy to propose a major change in organisation as a cure for company ills. If the business is centrally controlled they decentralise it, and vice versa; if the business is organised on a product basis they reorganise it on a geographic basis, and so on.

There are sometimes circumstances when an unsuitable

organisational structure is the cause of company problems. If there are overlapping functions and no clear lines of responsibility, or if an essential function is so placed in the structure that its executives lack the authority to do their jobs effectively, then changes must be made. Similarly, if the structure is out of balance so that one function dominates, or particular facets of the business are overvalued at the expense of others, a change of structure may be required to redress the balance. Also, as indicated earlier, if the company is changing direction a new structure may be necessary to take account of the changing demands of the new situation. But, sometimes, to change the structure is an easy option and is done as an *alternative* to evolving a new strategy.

Of course, if a structure is clearly unsuitable for carrying out the business plan, it must be amended; but no structure is absolutely right and, in a complex business, every conceivable type of structure will have its weaknesses and can be accepted only as a compromise.

This is especially true of a business operating in several countries, producing separate ranges of technically complex products. Should the primary subdivision of such a business be by function? Should it be by national entity or geographical region? Or should it be by product group? Each of these possibilities will have its advocates; each will certainly have some strengths and weaknesses. A functional structure may result in difficulties in the relationship between the technical and marketing functions within a territory. A geographic split may lead to duplication of resources and over-extended product ranges. The arguments for and against any of the alternatives are finely balanced and any of them will give rise to some operational problems.

Two- and even three-dimensional matrix organisations have been adopted to deal with problems of this kind and they do solve some of them, but only at the expense of complexity, dilution of personal responsibility, and, perhaps, a swollen cadre of staff appointees. There are no perfect solutions.

In summary, therefore, it is necessary to be on the alert for the need to develop an organisational structure which takes account of changes in business strategy, but to guard against such change being regarded as a panacea to cure deeper underlying problems.

Job specification

When the organisational structure required for the business has been decided, the primary tasks of the major organisational units can be defined in accordance with the strategy and objectives of the business. This makes it possible to draw up job specifications which will set down the objectives for each of the executives within the structure.

In an existing business there will, of course, already be a structure and one can assume that, unless there has been a radical change in policy, most of the existing managers will have relatively minor changes in responsibility. Occasionally, however, when for instance a new division is being created, a totally new set of management relationships has to be built up.

It is self-evident that each executive appointed should have experience and training which matches the requirements of the job specification. Yet, it is often tempting to appoint to a job a man who is considered to have great general ability, and assume that he will learn the job content while carrying it out. It is certainly true that if a job requires a particular functional expertise, a good manager will learn whatever is required. But this will be just theoretical knowledge, and it will take a long time before he acquires the almost instinctive feel for a situation that an experienced practitioner has. As a management team depends to a large extent for its success and cohesion on the respect its members have for the competence of their colleagues, an obvious learner in their midst is likely to be regarded as a weak link and become an irritant and cause of frustration.

On the whole, therefore, in making a new appointment I would not regard high general ability, in itself, as an adequate substitute for specific job knowledge. This is one of the reasons why it is important for any executive to gain diverse experience early in his career, so that the widening of responsibility that comes with promotion does not plunge him into unknown fields of expertise, but merely brings him back in contact with those that he practised earlier in his career.

The other obvious requirements are that each incumbent should have the ability to perform the judgemental and intellectual tasks of his job, to make a strong and respected contribution to the deliberations of his colleagues, and to be an effective leader of his own management team. Here the risk is the opposite to the one referred to earlier. A man may have been selected primarily for his job knowledge but be without the necessary level of ability to gain respect from his subordinates.

Personality

The effect of personality on a management team's work is a topic often discussed. Obviously an individual with personality defects that prevent him from building an acceptable working relationship with his colleagues has no place in a management team. Certainly, no one is entirely without irrational attitudes and reactions, so that the concepts of normal or abnormal personality need handling with some care. But there are some people so ill at ease with themselves that they are unable to accept any form of critical comment, or to enter any relationship without striving for dominance, or to develop any real group loyalty. Such people can have very high standards of intellectual ability and some of them may be very successful at the head of a small enterprise, despite the misery they may inject into the working lives of their subordinates. Within a larger team, such individuals are potentially so damaging to the integrity of the team that, whatever their ability, they should not be placed in positions of responsibility and authority.

Apart from such extremes, I am not convinced that personality factors have a decisive influence on the success of a management| team. Generally a man is accepted on the basis of his abilities and, if those are considered adequate, his idiosyncrasies are likewise accepted. It is only when the idiosyncrasies become dominant that they lead to problems in group relationships.

I am not sure that there is any satisfactory way of finding out, in advance, who such people are. Personality tests of various kinds have their proponents and there is some correlation between the results of the better tests and the observed behaviour of the individuals tested, but it is still imperfect. Such tests, therefore, support but do not replace personal judgement.

The chief executive must be sure that the important roles in his management team are filled by people in whom he has confidence and with whom he can work well. This means also (unfortunately) that they should fit the cultural and behavioural prejudices of the chief executive. There is nothing worse than a manager (however competent) who constantly irritates the chief executive and hence invites him to be unfair and unjust, or even to persecute him. It is easy to say that the chief executive should not react in such a way but most are fairly human and it is so easy for a personality clash to disrupt an otherwise cohesive team. There is much room in an effective management team for differences of opinion; there is no room for clashes of personality.

Team-leading

There is only one basis for effective team-leading and that is professionalism. It was and still is possible for a basically untrained manager to run a successful business. But less and less so. An increasing number of managers, well trained in the disciplines of their profession, are found at the top of major enterprises and, by their competence, are exerting pressures on those less adequately trained. No doubt, for a while yet, some successes will still be generated by untrained men of unusually high innate standards of judgement and ability; but such men are rare and, with the increasing availability of formal management training, will become rarer.

Qualities important for the success of a chief executive are:
1   A wide knowledge of management principles and experience of their practical application in a variety of situations.

2   A scientific approach.
3   Intellectual honesty.
4   A personal code of ethics which enables him to trust
     other people and in turn be trusted by them.
5   The ability to maintain discipline by example and by
     explicit action.

None of these factors can be a substitute for innate
personal authority, but that is a quality possessed by few
and only randomly attached to real ability. Its relevance in
the total business sense is, therefore, minimal.

Knowledge of management principles

Now that management has become a respectable subject for
advanced education and academic research, the sheer volume
of new material is far beyond the capacity of one man to
absorb. It is, however, necessary for a chief executive to keep
abreast of the main streams of management thought. I am
aware that many practical managers consider that the
theoretical work of the business schools has little relevance
to the hard day-to-day world in which they compete. But
most of those who take this attitude accept the theoretical
concepts of yesterday, second-hand, as part of received
wisdom.

In reality, many of the standard management tools could
only have been developed on the basis of theoretical study
and not from 'practical considerations'. One good example is
in the use of statistical methods for stock management. The
advantages of statistical techniques in optimising the balance
between the holding and levels of service is incontrovertible.
All concepts used, without which many companies could not
now operate effectively, were not evolved from direct
experience, but from specific study and investigation.

Even in the human relations field, where direct personal
experience has failed and the researches of behaviourists may
modern industry prevents the application of that experience
where it is most needed. Here too, the application of practical
experience has failed and the re-searches of behaviourists may
be the best hope of resolving, in the long term, conflicts that
seem inherent in large-scale industry.

There is, thus, an increasing amount of theoretical understanding and methodology that can only be learned through
systematic study because it would take too many lifetimes
to acquire it from experience and practical observation.

The chief executive, therefore, needs to be familiar with
the main streams of management thought. In practice, for
a young ambitious executive, a business school education is
very desirable and, for an older executive, who learned his
profession before the business school explosion, regularly
reading business magazines of the calibre of the *Harvard
Business Review* could be one way of keeping up-to-date.
As far as the specific application of new techniques is concerned,
one must guard against uncritical acceptance. The more practical
experience the chief executive has had in differing situations, the
more disconcerning he will be in adapting new ideas to his needs.

A secondary reason for acquiring a knowledge of management principles is the need for the chief executive to earn any
respect due to him within the top management team. If there
are obvious and important gaps in his management understanding, he will correspondingly forfeit some of it.

A scientific approach

All of us behave in irrational ways. It is part of human nature
to do so. A scientific attitude has existed for no more than
about ten generations and has become widespread only in the
last two, so that it is hardly surprising that a scientific approach
to management would be an acquired habit rather than an
innate characteristic.

In a management context the scientific approach is made
up of a number of elements, namely:

1   The use of quantified data   One thing that distinguishes
an effective organisation is the attempt to base all decisions
on objective data and, as far as possible, to quantify each
element of information, e.g. the assessment of economic
trends, market sizes, market share by segment, productivity
of people or capital, etc. But the scientific approach can go
much further than the consideration of simple data of this

kind. One extension is the use of statistical techniques to determine the probability of events whose individual occurrence is not capable of precise forecasting (quality defects, being out of stock of a product, having to wait more than a predetermined time for a service, etc). Quantifying everything possible has three important benefits:

1   It isolates and highlights the element of judgement in the conversion of a series of observations into a systematic relationship and so enables that judgement to be verified.
2   Once the judgement has been made it allows mathematical analogies and reasoning processes to be used, which are much more powerful than their verbal counterparts.
3   It is also a prerequisite for systematic planning.

2   Systematic planning process   The second element of a scientific approach is the preparation, from the objective data, of a systematic plan of action with a predicted outcome. This has been referred to in the previous chapter.

3   Systematic and objective performance review   The third element of the scientific approach is the measurement of what has happened against the plan, and the use of the comparison to improve the performance of individual aspects of the business and of individual executives. Where this is done each executive knows that he will be judged by performance and, because he has a plan and a set of objectives, he can himself assess his performance against these standards. He will normally have played a large part in setting his objectives and, therefore, there should be few disagreements about whether or not they have been achieved. This will, therefore, be considered an inherently fair way of assessment. Its use also applies self-discipline to the executives concerned. Where such processes are not available and an executive is judged by qualitative assessment alone, it is easy to get a totally wrong impression of his contribution. It is not the man who presents the most effective image who will necessarily achieve the most satisfactory results. Yet, it is so very easy to mistake the image for the substance and reward the man who is good at self-advertisement rather than the one

who quietly gets on and does an effective job without making
a fuss about it.

Intellectual honesty

Major business failures have often been signalled to all
concerned for years before the final collapse, but the signals
were ignored by the responsible managers, with the result
that shareholders and the employees of those companies
suffered accordingly. In most cases the managers were not
stupid. They certainly had enough intelligence to recognise
the signals and interpret them. Neither were the managers
consciously dishonest, but many of them appeared to have
lacked the ability to accept unpalatable facts and so they
brushed them aside until they were beyond concealing, and
also unfortunately beyond reversal.

Unwillingness to recognise, accept and examine unpalatable
information is one aspect of intellectual dishonesty.

Another form of intellectual dishonesty is that practised
by almost all party politicians: the presentation of a case for
a certain course of action using all the arguments that come
to hand, regardless of whether they are truly relevant or not,
and disregarding all the counter-arguments. A manager may
passionately believe that a particular future policy is right
for the business, and so he sets about to win acceptance for
that policy using fair means or foul. In the end, the decision
is not taken on its merits, but on his skill as an advocate.

So all too often it is the best debater who wins his point,
rather than the man whose views are really relevant to the
situation. Few policies in business are absolutely right or
absolutely wrong. If any manager vehemently supports or
opposes a policy to the extent of being blind to opposing
considerations, then that manager is an unreliable subordinate
and a dangerous colleague.

I do not suggest that every decision can be made on the
basis of objective facts alone. There are never enough facts
and there is never enough time to gather all that are available.
What is being suggested is that those that are available and
can be assembled economically should be examined as

objectively as possible. Any element of judgement necessarily exercised in order to reach a conclusion should be recognised as such.

Anyone who has worked for a manager with whom it was not possible to hold objective discussion knows how frustrating this can be. The subordinate never knows whether his senior has some specific reason for adopting a particular policy or whether it is the expression of some general dogma. He feels that his own ideas are overridden, not because of their inherent quality, but because they do not conform with his senior's personal prejudices. If he wants to retain his self-respect he will go and work somewhere else where he hopes his ideas will be given the respect due to them.

Another aspect of intellectual honesty is willingness to be self-critical. Within any group of people whose work interacts, there is a tendency for each individual to look at the work of the others and to find fault with it so as to account for whatever goes wrong. It takes a great degree of self-discipline to examine and criticise one's own performance first. This is a far more constructive attitude, but will never occur of its own accord, nor arise as a result of an instruction from the top. If, however, the chief executive always refuses to discuss criticism of other departments until a manager has first examined objectively the performance of his own department, self-analysis will become a standard practice that will open the door to a constructive analysis of a total situation.

Correcting mistakes

The chief executive's reaction to mistakes will strongly influence the attitude of his subordinates.

When he makes mistakes himself, he should admit them. He may feel that in doing so he is confessing to a weakness that will cost him respect and undermine his authority, but the reverse is true. He will earn respect by doing so. His criticism of other executives will be much more readily accepted, because there will be no suggestion that he is applying standards to them that he would not apply to himself. When he feels that it is necessary to hold firm to a particular decision in the face of adverse pressures, his subordinates will know that he is doing it because he believes the course is right rather than because he does not want to admit that it was wrongly chosen in the first place. They will be much more likely to go on giving him their full support than would otherwise be the case.

If he realises that he has done something unjust he should also be willing to admit it and correct the situation. Of course, it is better not to be unfair in the first place, but under pressure it is easy to react to superficial events rather than fundamentals.

The same rule applies to minor events as well as major ones; an unfair reproof is not materially as damaging as an unfair dismissal, but if it happens it should still be acknowledged and corrected.

A subordinate's mistakes also require careful handling. Should he ignore them, take the man quietly aside, carpet him, or send him irate memos? At times, all are appropriate. The only thing he must never do in any circumstances, even in the heat of the moment, is to critise him in front of his own subordinates. Minor mistakes should be ignored unless they come in droves, in which case either there is a fundamental misfit between the man and his job, or he has some personal problem. In both cases the man requires counselling, not reproof.

When a more serious mistake occurs, the chief executive should certainly discuss it in as dispassionate an atmosphere as possible, because it is important to find out why the mistake arose, and usually the executive concerned is as anxious to avoid a repetition as he is. If the problem is explored without any rancour, it may be easy to agree the cause. It may be that the executive needs training in certain aspects of his job, or perhaps it was an inexplicable one-off mistake such as we all make from time to time.

A formal censure is rarely appropriate unless it looks as if a man will have to be removed from his job, in which case it is desirable from a human as well as from a legal viewpoint to give a clear statement of the problem. Such a censure, which should be dealt with calmly in a face-to-face interview, should be supplemented by a letter setting out the main facts of the situation and explaining why it is necessary to avoid a repetition. The letter must be precise and blunt. It may be tempting to protect the man's feelings by suitable euphemisms that soften the criticism, but these should be avoided. Experience shows that when a formal censure is necessary it is rare that the executive can correct the situation, especially if there has been adequate counselling earlier. So the purpose of the letter and the warning is as much to give him some time to adjust to knowledge that his job is in danger, as it is to improve the situation. A 'kind' letter may still leave him thinking that all is well; and if there is a dispute about the fairness of any later action such a letter will certainly be regretted.

A personal code of ethics

It is important for a leader to be trusted. In the close community of a management team, a man's real attitudes and actions are readily separated from his public image, so the only way to be trusted is to ensure that promises and undertakings are scrupulously observed. It sometimes happens that an understanding given becomes an inconvenience. A manager may be tempted to use his authority to set aside such a commitment, perhaps to ignore it or deny that it ever existed. This may avoid a short-term difficulty but it is always harmful to the respect felt for the manager concerned and, if habitual, will undermine all confidence in him.

Once in a while, it is necessary to abrogate a commitment because circumstances have changed in such a fundamental way that to carry through the original decision would damage the business, or because it has been discovered that one premise upon which the commitment was based was plainly wrong. If this happens then an open admission of the circumstances is almost always more acceptable than any attempt at evasion.

Conversely, it is necessary to trust other people, particularly direct subordinates, unless there is an explicit reason not to do so and, in that case, the sooner the relationship is ended the better.

Obviously, honesty in discussion and behaviour are important, as is respect for other people's opinions and rights. Perhaps the most important need is willingness to sacrifice expediency for principle (not dogma).

I am well aware that many readers will be able to think of men who have been very successful in business and who, to say the least, have not been renowned for their observance of strict ethical rules of business conduct. I believe, however, that in today's management climate, in which consultation is replacing autocracy as an acceptable style, sound ethical standards have a practical effect on leadership ability, quite apart from any question of ethical behaviour as such.

Ability to maintain discipline

In every organised community there must be rules. These should be set at the minimum number necessary to achieve the objectives of the organisation and to contain interpersonal friction. Every manager should be looking for ways to eliminate unnessary regulations. The current move towards flexible hours in industry is a good example of the relaxation of earlier more rigorous demands of employers. But the rules which do exist must be enforced. There is nothing so disruptive as the existence of a privileged group apparently exempt from the normal codes of community behaviour.

Generally there are two ways to maintain discipline: example and authority. A good manager obeys the rules. The old precept: 'Don't do as I do, do as I say', has no place in a business management situation. Where rules are considered necessary, no one should be privileged to break them, because if any one person can do so, then everyone else can reasonably expect the same privilege.

For instance, in many companies the more senior people tend to arrive later than the official starting time. They would generally say, if challenged on this, that they work late regularly so it is quite reasonable for them to come in late. Unfortunately, it soon becomes accepted that the more senior a man is, the more free he is to ignore the normal starting time, so everyone who can get away with it arrives late and those who do arrive on time do very little work at the start of the day because they resent not having the same privilege. Lateness has become a status symbol!

If the chief executive spends the firm's money on private phone calls, or uses the xerox machine for his golf club circulars, he can certainly expect other people to follow, or to feel aggrieved if they are prevented from so doing.

The use of status in these and other ways as an excuse for breaking rules that need to be properly enforced is a particularly harmful habit. The first stage in preserving discipline is, therefore, that of example.

When example fails, then use of authority becomes essential. Managers often hesitate before calling in a subordinate and making a specific criticism of undesired practises. They forget that most people like to work in a structured environment. People will readily accept rules, provided that they understand why they are needed and believe that they are universally enforced; they will accept reproof when they break the rules as long as they know that the same would happen to anyone else. It is essential, therefore, that any rule of behaviour within a business should be universally enforced or cancelled.

Sometimes, cases arise in which an employee who is making a particularly strong contribution to one aspect of the business is ignoring company rules. The argument is advanced that, because he is an essential employee, he must be allowed latitude in his behaviour. This applies particularly to people occupying roles regarded as being creative. They are accorded 'artistic' license. I am not convinced that this is necessary or desirable. Of course, if 'creative' people are given an opportunity to gain preferential treatment they will accept it, but they will be most unlikely to walk out in high dudgeon if they are expected to observe normal standards of behaviour.

An interesting question on the matter of discipline is whether the chief executive should be 'one of the boys'? Should he participate in common leisure activities with his subordinates? This can be difficult to regulate, particularly if the chief executive is a man of a sociable disposition.

Whenever a company entertains its customers, the

executives concerned are participating in common social activities, and what is more natural than that this should spill over into leisure activities when outside guests are not present? The problem in such a situation is that the chief executive is in danger of creating a set of cronies who will be regarded, probably correctly, as having a special influence on his thinking. If he does not participate in any common leisure activities it will probably not reduce his management effectiveness, although if he applies such a rule rigidly it may certainly cause some resentment and give him a reputation of aloofness. Probably the best compromise is to participate in such activities sparingly and as far as possible on neutral ground — not at his own home or homes of his subordinates.

Purpose

The final characteristic of an effective leader, without which all the others are useless, is a sense of purpose. Many able administrators have all the other qualities, but they are not capable of directing the general course of a business. It is a paradox that, often, one of the qualities which inhibits their success is the very objectivity that has been discussed and praised earlier. They listen carefully to the views of their colleagues and subordinates as a good manager should and, when they are convinced that a particular policy is sound, they embark upon it. Later, when presented with another equally sound view, they try to follow that too, even though it may compete with the earlier decision. Sometimes, they may find that on the facts they cannot choose between two opposing policies, and then they may just let things slide and avoid making any decision. Nothing is more damaging to the respect held for the chief executive than the dithering, post-ponement of decisions, leaving things in the air, and lack of action which arise when he is too responsive to passing events.

This problem will arise because so often there is no single right policy for a particular business at a given time in its history. There is frequently a choice of several paths, each of which may, on the available facts, appear equally attractive. An effective team leader has to make his decision and then stand by that decision regardless of conflicting pressures. He may have to stand by it when trends seem adverse and when he is under strong pressure to change course. If there has been a real shift in the underlying circumstances, or if a new event has arisen to invalidate his earlier decision, then he must be ready to change course; but otherwise it is better to be too persistent than to change direction too readily.

A successful leader, therefore, must have enough sense of purpose to carry through his intentions despite the problems that will naturally arise on the way, but in the last resort enough flexibility to know when to discard his plan and start again. Unforeseen difficulties will arise in the course of execution of every conceivable plan. It is probably more harmful for the business to have a chief executive who is too willing to react to changing circumstances than one who is too inflexible. Sense of purpose is, therefore, a necessary attribute for a successful leader, and very valuable in achieving business success, provided that it stops short of sheer obstinacy.

Chairmanship

Many of the attributes of team leadership discussed in this chapter can be exemplified by the chief executive's approach to chairing a meeting.

Firstly, there must be an agenda. This might seem very obvious and so it is, but many executives will have experience of being called to meetings without having the slightest idea about what is to be discussed. A good chairman would never let this happen, even if it means disregarding his natural inclination to deal with the topic while it is on his mind or to strike while the iron is hot.

Preparation is also important for the chief executive himself. He must prepare for any meeting in advance, even if he feels that he is fully conversant with the matters to be discussed. He must know, in particular, what he hopes to get out of the meeting, whether he wishes to reach any formal conclusion, lay the foundation for a further investigation, or just get his subordinates' opinions for further consideration. He must make this clear before the meeting starts, because nothing is more frustrating for the participants than to go to a meeting expecting positive decisions and then to leave the meeting feeling that they are no further forward than before. If they know from the start that any actual decision will be taken later, and, better still, know why this is so, then they will be unlikely to react adversely.

The chairman must make sure that everyone at the meeting contributes. If anyone has nothing to contribute then he should not be there; but usually there are a few people at any meeting prepared to sit back and let other people do the talking and their views go by default. A good chairman will draw their contribution from them, if necessary by a question and answer session.

Meeting discipline is also important. It starts with simple things like setting and maintaining a timetable for the meeting, so that time is allocated to the really important topics and not frittered away on secondary considerations. The chairman must also be self-disciplined and resist the temptation to use the meeting to hold forth himself at length on each topic, rather than generate a true interchange of ideas. He must prevent discussion drifting off the topics on the agenda and prevent any individual dominating the meeting by the force of his views, or by his readiness to jump in at every gap in the discussion. In other words, he must ensure that there is a balanced discussion in which everyone participates, that it stays on the important topics on the agenda, and that it reaches whatever type of conclusion was intended.

Summary

The essential characteristics of an effective team leader are knowledge, objectivity, personal honesty, authority and sense of purpose. There is another characteristic mentioned earlier: innate personal authority. Without doubt it exists. There are people who have the art of attracting the enthusiastic support of other people almost regardless of the objectives being followed. I am not sure that such a characteristic has much relevance in an industrial managerial situation in which a man tends to be known by what he is, rather than by how he appears, but it is a factor that helps in the public relations aspects of a chief executive's job; so, if it is there, it is a positive factor, but in no way a substitute for the other qualities discussed in this chapter.

6 *Succession Planning*

It is a truism that the most important assets of a business are the people employed in it; more specifically, the quality and depth of management is the determinant of long-term success.

With the right management team all problems are soluble, and other forms of assets can be acquired. Even a company in dire financial trouble can be pulled back from the brink of insolvency by a management team that can inspire confidence in the company's creditors and bankers. The desirable attributes, such as a strong market position, a competitive product range, productive plant, a contented work-force, are the results of the work of an effective management team.

But a management team is essentially impermanent. Ambitious young managers will not be content to remain in one job too long. They will be looking for the next opportunity and, if the next step does not seem to be available within the company, they will look outside it. Any young and able manager, however well he is looked after, and however carefully the chief executive helps him plan his career progression, may be attracted by a tempting offer elsewhere.

But losses are, of course, not only the result of ambition. Illness and incapacity take their toll. Personal problems may deflect a manager's energies. Business growth may make a manager's job too big for him.

The problem is not just that there is an unavoidable and continuous loss of executives; it is also that the rate of loss is at its highest among the most able. Any company has and needs a mixture of skills and abilities. Creative thinkers and high achievers are essential, but so are safe, reliable organisation men to make sure that the management machine is an efficient instrument of management policy. The attitudes which go with the two types of managers are both wanted; but the losses will always tend to be higher with people in the former category just because they are the ones more likely to go out and find new jobs or, for that matter, to suffer heart attacks or to fall victim to other stress-induced illnesses. The result is that unless there is an *active* policy of succession planning a company may very easily come to be dominated by administrators who may crowd out the creative and thrusting minority among the team.

Initial management intake

The first requirement in succession planning is, therefore, to make sure that the company develops and nurtures a source of high achievers. How this will be done depends very much on the nature of the business and its size.

If the company has reason, in the normal course of its business, to employ people of high intellectual attainments, e.g. engineers, designers, accountants, business planners and the like, then there is a pool of general talent, within which the potential future managers can be identified and developed. If the company's operations are generally characterised by low skill requirements it may not be possible to select an adequate number of managers from amongst its employees and it may be necessary to arrange for a regular intake of management trainees.

Although the latter arrangement simplifies the recruitment problem because the objectives are explicit, I would usually prefer to obtain potential managers by selection from a general pool of employees, rather than by specific recruitment, for two reasons:

1   Management potential is one of the hardest qualities to evaluate at an interview, particularly at the beginning of a man's career. Men with strong personalities, who seem natural leaders, may be so; but they may just be good interviewees and lack the ability to make the right decisions when under pressure or when presented with conflicting pieces of evidence. Many of the most successful managers I have met did not impress me with their personality on first acquaintance. I am not certain that I would have selected them at an interview and, even knowing them and seeing them in action, I doubt whether I could always identify the source of their success. But they did have the art of making sensible decisions and getting them carried out.

Psychological aptitude tests and the contributions of graphology and other borderline disciplines may improve the chances of being right, but I am not convinced that any form of selection yet developed can do more than marginally improve the odds.

2   I am not at all sure that it is good for a company to have within it a cadre of management trainees. Other employees may well feel that for them the door to promotion has been shut, which means those who believe they have the ability to succeed in management will either leave, or operate in an attitude of resentful frustration. The management trainees may come to regard themselves as innately superior to other employees and fail to take account of the importance of the contributions of other members of the staff.

However, a company may have only the choice between recruiting management trainees to provide for the necessary long-term management succession, or to fill the majority of management jobs as they become vacant, from outside the company. In this situation, I would prefer the former. There are, therefore, circumstances in which it is essential to establish a management training group. However, when this is done, one needs to ensure that the trainees get their hands dirty, figuratively or otherwise, by carrying out the basic operations of the company and undertaking first-line supervisory responsibilities, before being appointed to more senior management positions, and their promotion must depend entirely on their performance in more junior roles. In essence, appointment as a management trainee must be regarded as a passport to an opportunity, not as giving the right to a certain status in the future.

The establishment of some kind of initial management selection process, either from existing staff categories or by special intake, ensures that there is depth of management, and that the company is, or will become, capable of filling most management jobs from within.

Promotion or recruitment

There is some argument about whether it is best to fill management jobs from within a company or from external recruitment. Some companies, particularly large groups, depend almost entirely on internal promotion. This certainly has the benefit of ensuring that the people appointed are already well known to the company and, therefore, unlikely to be conspicuously inadequate in their new roles. It has the further advantage that the managers understand, in some depth, the nature of the business in which they are operating, its management style and climate, its markets and products, and its general ethos. This ensures continuity of management methods.

The approach has weaknesses, however. The most important are that mediocrity may well become self-sustaining, or that a particular set of policies remains un-challenged, just because everyone has got used to them. It is also very easy to get used to malpractice within a business, and to treat it as the norm.

An outsider with a different experience and background to the executives within the company can often see more clearly the company's fundamental strengths and weaknesses, and can take a more objective view about future policies.

The position is analagous to someone regularly driving the same motor car. It gradually deteriorates: the steering gets looser, the engine gets noisier, the brakes less effective, and the proud owner may never notice that anything has changed

until he lends it to a friend. He has not consciously tolerated
any shortcomings; it is just that they have developed so
slowly that he has not noticed them. So it is with companies;
practices and policies can change imperceptibly and become
acceptable through familiarity. The outsider used to other
standards will be struck by what he sees as the company's
shortcomings.

If, however, too many senior management jobs are filled
from outside continuity is lost. It will take time before each
new executive fully understands the business, and in the
meantime he may well make decisions which are based on
too superficial a view.

It is my belief, therefore, that no company should recruit
all its senior executives from within; nor should it fill too
many top jobs from outside. A balance needs to be struck.
This very much depends upon the company's current situation
and recent history, but I would normally favour filling
between a half and three-quarters of senior management jobs
from within the company, and the remainder from outside.
This seems to provide the best balance between ensuring a
continuity of style, giving existing staff an opportunity for
advancement, and the injection of new ideas and attitudes.

The succession plan

Depth of management and the right mix between high
achievers and solid administrators provides a framework for
succession planning, but will not automatically ensure that
there is an adequate successor for each role. This requires a
succession plan.

To prepare one, a chief executive should start by mentally
assassinating each executive in turn starting with himself,
and deciding who would be the logical successor. The logical
successor may well not be the executive's second in command.
To illustrate this, let me quote the fate of a small engineering
company I was once concerned with as a management consultant. It had been started by an energetic entrepreneur. He was
primarily an engineer and recognising his weaknesses in the
administrative field, he hired a capable man, who had

previously worked for the accountancy firm who were his company's auditors, to look after this side of the business. The entrepreneur and his administrator (who in due course became his deputy) were a very successful partnership, the one inventing and developing new products, introducing changes and sometimes creating a good bit of confusion, the other picking up the pieces, smoothing down ruffled feelings and generally maintaining good order. They were going from strength to strength when the entrepreneur had a heart attack, soon to be followed by a second one, and was ordered by his doctor to retire. He then made the mistake of handing over the chief executive's role to his deputy. Five years later the business was still in existence, but only a shadow of its former self. It was well run, housekeeping was superb, the office systems and the administration were impeccable; in almost every textbook sense management was first-class. Only the balance sheet and the profit and loss account revealed the true picture: the business was dying. Too few products had been developed and these were only routine improvements on existing ones; margins on the older products were slipping away as they moved towards obsolescence. The founder's marketing methods were still being meticulously followed although circumstances had changed considerably and new distribution channels had grown in importance.

When the chief executive had to be replaced to save the business, he was bitterly resentful. He knew that he had managed competently; and so he had, in the only way he knew.

This illustrated a common difference between a chief executive and his number two. The chief executive is concerned primarily with entrepreneurial activities, in finding the right markets, building the right management team, securing financial resources, etc., and must not allow himself to be involved in too much detail. Generally it is his deputy who has to make sure that the details are taken care of. He requires different qualities from the chief executive. He must be involved in detail; he must be meticulous; he must be an organisation man; he must be an administrator, otherwise he would be in permanent conflict with number one. Therefore, if a nominated second-in-command exists, he may well be the wrong man to be the chief executive's successor, and it is more likely that one would be found amongst the main functional executives of a business.

Similarly, when considering succession in other key roles, the best man may not come from the department under review, but from elsewhere in the business.

In this way succession planning is closely interlinked with management development. Junior executives particularly need to be exposed to a variety of experience, and for this to be done in such a way that each job stretches them more than the previous one. This makes it desirable that when promotion prospects exist as wide a net as possible should be cast to find the right man. Ideally, there should be a choice of two or three potential successors for each position in the organisation.

Looking at things from the point of view of the executives concerned, there may be more than one logical next career step. This will be specially true of those in more junior roles. This can provide considerable flexibility of action when plans have to be implemented.

Too rigid a succession plan will always fail, and succession planning is a bit like planning future moves in a game of chess; a plan for several moves ahead must always exist in the player's mind, but what he actually does must depend on his opponent's moves as well. In succession planning the opponent (fate, luck, call it what you will) also makes his moves, always at the wrong time and success depends on having the right pieces in the right positions to mount an effective counter-play.

Consideration of structure

In practice when succession is being planned, or when a succession problem arises, it may be found necessary to change the structure. Any management structure, however carefully worked out to suit the needs of the business, tends to be distorted by the abilities of the people working within it. There is no such thing as a perfect fit in any executive role. A very good executive will still have his weaknesses and particular fields of strength. If the latter apply to mangement areas normally covered by other functions he may, in the course of time, acquire some responsibilities which would have been allocated elsewhere in a conventional structure. As an example, the industrial engineering department usually reports to the manufacturing manager of a business because the role of such a department is to minimise manufacturing cost. If, however, the chief design engineer happens to have had good manufacturing experience, and is conscious of the cost aspects of design and, therefore, concerned with production methods, he may become responsible for industrial engineering.

All structures, without exception, become distorted in this kind of way. There exists, therefore, the danger that when considering succession, duties and responsibilities of a job are defined in accordance with the present, distorted, structure, not with what would be the optimum structure. It is necessary, therefore, to go back to first principles and not just ask whether someone can be found to fulfill the role of the last incumbant of the position, but to determine what the organisational structure should be like and whether someone in the company could fill the job as it would be in that 'ideal' structure.

I have stressed that a change of structure is a valid solution to a company's problems only if there has been a significant change in the circumstances in which it operates. In succession planning, however, temporary structural innovation may be an appropriate way of resolving succession problems. One example of this is the fact, mentioned earlier, that all structures are modified by the personal qualities of those working within them. The appointment of a new executive automatically affects the structure to some extent.

A more deliberate use of structural modification, for the purpose of succession planning, is the creation of temporary roles. These may give an up-and-coming executive specific experience, as when a project team is established and an executive is given the responsibility for the project.

Another appropriate use of temporary roles for the purpose of succession planning concerns executives nearing retirement age. In most companies there are projects for which experience and judgement are more important than energy and innovative spirit and it may be appropriate to assign an older executive to such a project in the last year or two of his employment. This will give an opportunity for his successor to move into the job at the right time in his career, rather than be left for two years cooling his heels and possibly becoming disaffected. Such a temporary assignment may also be very acceptable to the older executive, who may welcome the stimulation of a new challenge and of new interests at this stage of his career.

Summary

Of all the steps a chief executive can take to improve the performance of his business and reduce pressures on himself, getting the right management team is perhaps the most rewarding. When this is done well, there is an almost tangible lift in the spirit of the organisation as each fits into his new role and starts to make an impact on it. The knowledge that one more department is in competent hands has a most direct effect on the workload of the chief executive and his ability to concentrate on the really essential factors.

He can then stop fire-fighting and start to do the real jobs of the chief executive, one of these being to produce a succession plan which will do much to safeguard the company's future by ensuring that it continues to have a good management team.

7 Management Style

Why think about management style at all? Would it not be better just to behave naturally? If a management style is self-consciously adopted, does this not create a barrier of artificiality between the chief executive and his subordinates? If a manager tries to behave in ways that do not come naturally to him, will that not create an awkwardness in his approach which will limit his effectiveness? Is not the adoption of a particular management style an attempt to create an artificial personality, which, in itself, is likely to undermine the trust and respect the chief executive needs if he is to be really effective?

I think not. On the contrary, I believe that a conscious effort to select and develop a particular management style throughout an organisation is one of the hallmarks of a competent and effective chief executive. A management style is necessarily artificial, because the management situation is itself artificial. A chief executive has to reach out beyond his immediate subordinates and influence the way the whole business is managed. People are just not programmed to do that naturally. Instead they tend to be most skilled at relating to, and influencing, a small group of people with whom they are in immediate daily contact. It does not come naturally to most people to do more than that and it is an art to be learned and developed by anyone who aspires to run a successful organisation in any field.

The situation is rather analagous to that of the theatre. If the actors were to come on stage and address each other exactly as they would in real life their message would not get beyond the first two or three rows of the stalls and even that would be muted beyond understanding. To convey their message they have to project an image which is larger than life.

A chief executive has a similar problem. He has to reach out beyond the people with whom he is in day-to-day contact and get his message through to a wider audience and, unlike the actor, he has to do it largely through intermediaries and can rely only minimally on the projection of his own personality. It is a difficult job but a very necessary one, because:

1   It strongly influences the way policies are carried out — with enthusiasm or with acquiescence.
2   It has a profound influence on the state of industrial relations within the company.
3   It determines whether the creative energies of all the employees are harnessed in the company's interest.

It is perhaps dangerous to carry the theatre analogy too far because the chief executive is trying to create an *attitude* that will permeate the whole business and is certainly not just trying to project his own *personality*.

Need for consistency

If he fails to adopt a coherent style and just reacts to situations as he feels would be appropriate at the time, then he will respond differently from day to day, and his response will depend on many factors which have nothing to do with the business situation facing him. If he is feeling relaxed, for example, he may be openly receptive to subordinates' ideas, just because he has time to reflect on them. Another day he may be very busy and perhaps have some problems on his mind, and brush aside any ideas that conflict with his own immediate intentions. He will appear inconsistent and his subordinates will not know how they are expected to behave with him. Yet he may not feel any inconsistency. He may not even be aware that he is creating any problems; on the contrary he may feel that his relationships are excellent because he behaves 'naturally'. But he is the chief executive and, like it or not, he represents his office and authority.

A consistent management style leads to predictability. If a chief executive influences his subordinates to adopt a similar style then there will be consistency of behaviour within the management team which will reinforce its effectiveness in influencing attitudes within the company. Gradually it will become part of the culture of the organisation, to the extent that anyone not conforming will feel discomfort and move elsewhere, so the style becomes self-perpetuating.

My point is that the way in which a manager presents his ideas and decisions and gets them carried out influences his success almost as much as the quality of those ideas and decisions, because the presentation — the style — will determine the kind of response he will get from his subordinates. The effects are far-reaching and it is important to get it right.

Autocratic management style

Most companies started with an autocratic management style. A man starts a business and it is *his* business in a very personal sense. He is the boss. All problems come to him. He makes all the decisions. Most small companies are like that. Usually, there is not room for more than one set of basic ideas or one decision-maker. If such a business grows fast the management style can persist, although it usually goes through a number of crises at various stages of growth. The first comes when the business gets so large that the chief executive is physically unable to take all the decisions and is forced to delegate some part of his responsibilities. He often finds men who are willing to execute policy without having a say in its formulation. To a very large degree they act as an extension of the boss's personality referring everything of importance to him.

If he goes on taking the right business decisions and

negotiating the right deals, this style can be a formula for very rapid growth indeed. Its weakness emerges from a number of possible events:

1   The external environment changes. The chief executive is so busy that he has no time to notice it, until his company results look sick. Then he may find himself in a position where his own formula for success has been found wanting, but he may be temperamentally incapable of consulting anyone else about the reasons for this. In any case he has probably driven out of the organisation anyone who wanted to play any part in policy-making.

2   An even more serious crisis develops when the chief executive becomes old or ill, and often is unwilling to admit there is any deterioration in his abilities. Nothing is more symptomatic of disaster ahead than when an octogenarian finally gives up the reins to his already elderly son.

One need not be an autocrat isolated from the common herd to have delusions of infallibility. Success can engender them too. Success is usually the result of a combination of a man's ability and the opportunity that presented itself. Sometimes it may indeed be that the opportunity was so outstanding that the man succeeded despite himself. But he may be totally convinced that it is entirely due to some special talent of his or to his unique method of approach, applicable to all situations. He may then act in a similar fashion in entirely different circumstances, only to dissipate the fruits of his original venture. And the aura of his success may then have shut the mouth of any potential critic.

In the aftermath of the last war there was a shortage of building plant, and one ingenious engineer had the bright idea of using some of the surplus war material to build lorry-mounted cranes. The chassis were from redundant military trucks, the crane slewing rings had been originally made for tank gun turrets and much of the hydraulic gear came from similar sources. Most competitive products had two engines, one for the vehicle and one for the crane. But these engines were expensive, so he came up with the idea of driving the crane through a hydraulic pump mounted on the vehicle gearbox; in doing so he was able to dispense with one of the engines.

His cranes were a great success. They were robust, efficient and cheap and his hydraulic drive arrangement was initially unique. He was able to build up his business very rapidly, giving his competitors a hard time. As the business developed over the years, his formula for success remained unchanged: crude but reliable engineering, low overheads, keen prices, and keeping very close to the men who actually drove the cranes.

He acquired quite a reputation for business acumen. But he was unprepared for a new technical break-through that happened in the industry and required more sophisticated engineering than his company was capable of providing. He tried to cobble together cranes to satisfy the new requirements but only to be faced with several failures in the field. Despite desperate attempts to save the business, it had eventually to be financially reconstructed. Here was a firm whose development was arrested because it was too successful too soon. Several executives of the company had at various times expressed their apprehension about the future, but the managing director had been able to still their criticism and it had been the fact that he was such an obviously successful businessman which more than anything else had reassured them.

Often such chief executives maintain a very wide gulf between themselves and their immediate subordinates. If they want advice or comment about a particular situation they ask for it. If they do not ask, then they do not expect it to be offered. They react to gratuitous advice as an affront to their position. Chief executives who develop such a relationship with their immediate subordinates behave in other ways as if gulf in status equals gulf in ability. They regard subordinates as people to be given instructions, to be guided to adopt sound attitudes, to be criticised for errors, to be patronised and to be guarded against heresy. Often a master-servant relationship is much in evidence.

As indicated earlier this kind of situation is most in evidence where a business is family-owned or has grown rapidly under the influence of a single energetic entrepreneur.

If such a business does not succumb at one of the earlier growth barriers and if the chief executive maintains his personal authority until it is a large organisation, a management crisis is eventually almost inevitable. When the founder finally gives up control, the deterioration of performance can be very rapid, and because there are no home-grown managers fit to take over, the business tends to be very vulnerable to a takeover.

An autocratic management style can be extremely effective and lead to rapid growth, but it is a very difficult style with which to run a major enterprise and many men have worn themselves out in the attempt.

Committee management

At the other extreme and only in large organisations, there may be committee management. The chief executive behaves as the first among equals and acts almost as a neutral chairman, interpreting committee decisions. As few deliberations of committees result in rapid action or creative decisions the weakness of an approach of this kind is self-evident.

It is very easy, however, for committees to grow and for committees to assume that they have some kind of executive status. Committees are, after all, essential. There must be some kind of group communication in order to coordinate activities and to exchange ideas. The problem arises when there are too many committees, particularly, as so often happens, when their functions overlap and when their members fail to realise that their role is essentially advisory. In the end an executive has to make up his mind and take a personal decision without recourse to any reference to a 'majority view' should things go wrong.

Participation

If I reject autocratic management as having a low survival value and reject committee management because the result is usually mediocre, why not advocate participation?

It is fashionable today to consider that many of the ills of industry could be eliminated by greater participation by all employees in management decisions. It is noticeable that most of the people who advocate such solutions are themselves not actively involved in business management. Most of them are politicians, trade union officials, or academics. The reason why businessmen rarely advocate participation is easy to see. They feel that their own power to manage their companies is being handed over to the shop-floor activists who are more concerned with short-term benefits than the long-term success of the enterprise. Indeed, some are presumed to be positively hostile to the whole economic system within which the enterprise operates.

This is a biased view of course. It is by no means certain that, if true participation were possible, extremists would seize control; but what is true is that the advocates of participation tend to disregard a great deal of what we know about human nature and the nature of power in any organisation.

Full participation, in which every person who may be affected by a decision has some say in its formulation, will probably always remain very rare in industry. Ever since industrialisation began, there have been cooperative ventures based on the principles of participation, but these have all lost their purity as soon as they have started to grow. All large cooperatives have assumed most of the organisational attitudes and structures of more typical companies. They have had to in order to survive. There is a very clear negative correlation between a participative management style and the size of the organisation: in small groups full participation is possible, in large groups it is not. This is because the majority of people positively need leadership. They are not just *content* to be organised, they *want* to be organised.

All forms of society have depended on positive leadership by individuals, and all complex societies have adopted some form of hierarchy in which a large majority is content to be organised by a minority. The trades unions are a classic example of this. In their case participation is a fundamental aspiration, and yet a very small percentage of members actually participate in the running of trades unions. In the case of such voluntary organisations the failure of members to participate in management is often deplored because it may allow a small group of activists, often with narrow and specific aims, to take control of the organisation and lead it down paths quite inappropriate to the aspirations of its members. This refusal to participate is not, however, just an example of perversity on the part of the non-participators, it is a thoroughly entrenched human characteristic.

The evolutionary advantage of the willing acceptance of leadership is quite apparent. Any group that did not practice it would have been very rapidly extinguished by competitive forces. Whether we like it or not, the habit of hierarchical leadership has been bred into us and is a fundamental element of our existence. Participation, although a laudable objective, will always be a minority taste.

Perhaps this is just as well. If every decision had to be discussed in advance with all the people and have the approval of the majority before it could be implemented then no large organisation could exist. A hierarchy is what gives sense and purpose to a large number of individuals. A leaderless group is a mob that has great powers for destruction but none whatever for constructive purposes.

I take it as axiomatic, therefore, that any organisation requires positive leadership, that men are programmed by their inheritance to accept such leadership and that only a minority wish actively to participate in management decisions. If it were not so then large organisations could not exist because their whole energies would be spent making decisions and nothing would be left for implementation. Despite all the populist talk about participation, the existence of any large organisation depends on the exercise and the acceptance of authority.

The underlying motive for claims for active participation is, however, a strong one; it can easily be shown that, historically, the first interest of employers has not been the welfare of the employees. Indeed, decisions are being taken all the time which seek to preserve the success of the business as an entity, at the expense of certain groups of its employees. An obvious example arises at the time of a recession; a fall in sales volume may reduce cash flow to such an extent that a reduction of expenditure becomes the overriding management priority. A redundancy programme may be one way of achieving this. When this happens, the employees may think that had the business been better managed they would not have been made redundant. If the business has been successful in the past, the employees may feel that the shareholders should make the sacrifice and accept lower profits, or losses, in order to preserve employment through the recession (which is always seen as temporary).

In reality, this is not usually a valid possibility, because it is more often a cash crisis than a profit crisis that puts a company into liquidation during difficult trading times, and when a company is in trouble it can be very hard to get more cash.

I also have considerable doubt that more participation could even theoretically help to avoid the crises which often beset companies. In most cases, the management team are conscientiously doing their best to make the company successful. If problems arise they seek to resolve them to the best of their ability and judgement. If they reject alternative ways of running their company it is usually because they believe that the alternative ways are not suitable. Above all, they believe that the crisis in which the company finds itself is due to external causes which they have done everything possible to overcome. They may be mistaken in this, but their failure is rarely due to lack of effort or concern, although it may well be due to lack of ability.

Consultative management style

I reject, therefore, the current tendency to advocate greater participation as the cure for industrial relations problems, because I think that participation as a word and as a concept casts too wide a net for what I have in mind, although I respect the attitude of those who regard it as ethically desirable. In its place I would favour a consultative style of management. It seems to me desirable that anyone whose job may be affected to any important degree by a management decision should be consulted before that decision is taken.

100

Consultation seems to have value for two main reasons:

1   It is foolish to pretend that management has the mono-
     poly of wisdom. During the course of consultation there
     is a likelihood that ideas may be generated which may
     present a better solution to a problem under discussion
     than that initially envisaged.
2   People more readily accept change after they have been
     consulted than if they have not had the opportunity
     to contribute. This applies even if the final decision is
     not in accordance with their own views.

Obviously, the extent to which people want to be consulted
varies considerably depending on the kind of work they are
engaged in. In departments carrying out routine work *most*
employees just want to get on with work and not be bothered
with decisions about it. They do not particularly like change
and all they want is minimum disturbance of established
routines. People like this are in the majority and they will
not thank anyone for forcing them to contribute towards
decisions. There will, however, be a small number of people
in such departments who do want to be involved, and a good
manager knows who they are and, before making changes,
will talk things through with them. It is this type of continuous,
largely informal, dialogue that leads to the kind of relationship
within the company in which management authority can be
exercised and the generation of change accomplished without
severe conflict.

In departments engaged in creative work there is likely to
be a bigger proportion of people who want to be able to
present their views, but the principles remain the same: good
informal consultation builds the trust that enables management to operate effectively.

In addition to the informal practices there is a need for
formal consultative procedures to enable elected representatives of employees to discuss matters of interest with management. Most large companies today have works councils
although they are not so common in small organisations.
Success in operating these depends crucially on management's
attitudes to consultation. If management has established a
works council because it genuinely believes that the process
of consultation can lead to better decisions by management,

101

and if it believes that the communication of ideas in both directions can lead to more effective implementation of policies, then it will prove valuable.

If, however, it is set up just to defuse a potentially explosive labour situation — 'to keep them quiet' — or as a formal response to a theoretical acceptance of the need for consultation, then it will almost certainly fail and degenerate into a mere complaints committee.

One thing is certain, success in this field depends almost entirely on management attitudes. Management must ensure that every proposal put forward at a meeting is taken to its conclusion, on its merits. If this is done, then the representatives at the meeting will believe that it has value. If the proposals are left in the air or if people get the feeling that any of their proposals are opposed on principle, the council will soon be recognised as a talking shop and treated as such.

In my view, it is important that a company provides the opportunity and the means for those who wish to take an active part in planning and controlling their own work situation to do so. Far from weakening management authority, effective consultation will considerably improve management's ability to initiate and implement change.

Developing a management style

A consultative attitude can be created only from the very top of an organisation and by a continuous process of training and education. Only the chief executive can decide to adopt this particular style of management and only he has the power to have it implemented. It all starts with the chief executive's personal example. I believe that he should adopt a structured open-door policy. Any senior executive should have easy access to the chief executive. I use the word 'structured' because I do not want to imply that anyone should be free just to walk straight in. No one should have to suffer that sort of fragmentation of his working day. But every senior executive should have an opportunity to make a readily available appointment.

Every executive should feel free to express any new ideas

or any doubts and reservations about a course being followed, without being snubbed or criticised if the views he expresses do not accord with the views of the chief executive himself. It is perhaps pressing human nature too hard to suggest that the chief executive should especially welcome views that are contrary to his own — but he should try. It is so very easy to close one's mind to anything that suggests one's own cherished plans are not destined to success and to recognise the adverse influences only when they are beyond concealment. An open door and an open mind may at least help to ensure that the risks are identified early and counter-measures are taken while the problems are still small enough to be contained.

It is, of course, no good having a management style just for the chief executive. It must permeate the organisation; a chief executive not only has to keep an open door himself, but he must also encourage his subordinates to do the same in their own departments and ensure as far as possible that they are as receptive to the ideas of their subordinates. Equally, it is important that a consultative style is an expression of real respect for other people's ideas rather than just a technique to ensure good industrial relations.

Does this mean that a chief executive can employ only managers who subscribe to his own views? That helps. What happens if a chief executive joins a company that already has a full management team, with its own management style and its own ethos? The short answer is that if he dislikes it he should change it. That is what he is there for. Firstly, he changes it by practising the style he is preaching. Then he encourages his executives to do the same. Many will start by being extremely sceptical that any good will come from consulting their subordinates about decisions they are making, but if they start, even under pressure from the chief executive, they will find it works. They will learn that some of their subordinates want to be involved in wider business decisions and can make a constructive contribution. They will find that a consultative style not only helps them to make better decisions, but also to appreciate which members of their staff have the capacity for development and promotion and which are content to stay at their existing levels. Such findings are important for the company and also for the men concerned; nothing damages a man's health and happiness more than being appointed to a position that he is not adequate to undertake.

What happens if, after the example and the persuasion, the chief executive finds that one of his executives will not adopt his new style? I put that question at a public seminar long ago to a famous American company doctor. His answer was: 'Fire the bastard!'. At the time I questioned this. It seemed to me that if an executive was achieving the performance specified in the company's budget for his department, he had the right to manage the department in his own style. Now I am not so sure. I have come to the conclusion that consistency in management style is important. If the whole company is run in an autocratic style it can succeed (although I do not believe that it is the best way for running an organisation); but if one part is run in an autocratic way and another part in a consultative way the word soon spreads, comparisons are made, and those not permitted the luxury of consultation become restless and resentful. I believe, therefore, that whatever style a chief executive chooses, he must insist on its adoption as a basic factor of management policy and permit no major departures from it.

Am I preaching absolute conformity? It may sound so, but the point I am really making is that every employee should have an opportunity to put his views and get thoughtful response, whether favourable or unfavourable.

Consultation and decision-making

How does 'consultation' differ from 'participation'? It is a matter of who makes the decisions. Under a consultative management style every major topic is discussed fully with the executives concerned before the chief executive makes the decision based on his own judgement, having taken into account the views he has been given. It is the chief executive who takes the decision. If it is the same as the majority view, fine. But it is his job to make decisions and be responsible for them. The same goes for decisions taken at a lower level by other executives. If they are wise they will consult their subordinates and take account of the views that they are given. But they alone are accountable for the decisions they eventually make and must stand or fall by their success or failure.

This does not mean that everything has to be discussed in committee. In my experience it is very rare that important insights are gained during formal management meetings; that is much more likely to happen during speculative discussions not aimed at reaching specific decisions. It is, therefore, my belief that a chief executive should reserve time for regular informal discussions with his immediate subordinates. It must be clearly understood that anything relevant to the company's activities can be explored during these discussions without commitment to, or expectation of, a definite programme of action. Although a tight agenda for such discussions would vitiate their purpose, it is evident that each one must revolve around a selected key topic, to ensure that any interesting points that may emerge are followed through to a stage at which specific studies can be called for.

If the chief executive makes effective use of such dialogues with his senior managers, they will become increasingly aware of the main constraints on the company's progress, and of the policies necessary to deal with them. In this way a body of common understanding that will give a better foundation for the formal decision-making processes is built up amongst the management group.

It will be seen from the above that I do not believe that formal meetings are a good forum for the exploration of *fundamental* issues. The main reasons for this are that they are necessarily limited in time, that usually too many people are present, that there is too little opportunity for an individual to develop an argument from basic premises to a conclusion, and even less to consider seriously any counter-arguments. Such meetings can easily degenerate into a series of inconclusive discussions, or, worse, a series of decisions based on half-digested information.

The formal meetings of the management group have the important function of crystallising action programmes and monitoring performance. They will do that effectively only if the ground has been carefully prepared.

When there is an important decision to be taken it is worth while to take a lot of trouble to obtain a consensus among the top management group before formalising the decision. Executives who have been fully involved in making a decision which they feel reflects their own judgement will be wholeheartedly committed to ensuring that it is effectively implemented and that the predicted benefits are attained. However, the desirability of a consensus should not make us forget that it is the chief executive who must actually make the decision and be accountable for its outcome. Other executives, or a management committee, may submit proposals or give him advice. But even if there has been unanimous support for a decision, it is still the chief executive's decision and not one of a group of executives or of the committee.

It follows that there will be occasions when the chief executive will listen to the advice of his subordinates and say, in effect: 'I have listened to what you have said. I respect your views. But for these overriding reasons I have decided to take a different road.' This should not happen very often, because in most cases all the available facts should have been made available to everybody involved, with the implications thoroughly discussed and the decision emerging as a logical consequence of the evidence presented. But it may happen if there is a paucity of hard facts and if the argument for or against a course of action are based in the main on judgement, as, for example, when a company wants to enter a new field of business or launch a new product.

The chief executive is entitled to expect absolute commitment to the implementation of a decision, irrespective of how it has been made and whether there has been a consensus or not. There can be no question of any executive opting out, or giving only halfhearted support, on the ground that he thinks it was a wrong decision. Even a suggestion that this might be the executive's attitude will have an effect on the way the next line of executives implement his instructions. If, for instance, he were to say to his subordinates: 'This is what we have to do. I don't really agree with it, but this is what the boss wants', then the implementation will be half-hearted and the chance of a successful outcome seriously diminished.

If there has been a serious attempt to implement a decision and it turns out that it was a wrong one, then there should be no attempt by the chief executive to apportion blame. It is, after all, his responsibility alone. In any case, if he wants his subordinates to let him know truthfully what they really think about important topics, they must be certain that they can do so without being blamed if later events do not support their judgement.

Of course, this does not mean that he will not take note of the fact that an executive makes frequent errors of judgement and particularly so when this happens in pursuit of his functional duties or in the exercise of his line responsibilities. But that is a question of assessing the executive's competence in his specific role and not a matter for making him responsible for decisions which are rightly the responsibility of the chief executive.

Supporting subordinates

A chief executive must always support his executives. In public there should never be any hint that he is not fully in support of their decisions and actions. In private he should criticise them if he believes that something major is going wrong; but generally he should let them make their own decisions and intervene only if the results being achieved are not according to plan.

If an executive has problems and seeks advice it is obviously right for the chief executive to put his own views on the situation and on the best line of action to be followed. If the problem is entirely within the department of the executive concerned, the chief executive should leave it to him to decide what action to take. To do otherwise is to undermine the executive, and also remove any possibility of forming a true assessment of his ability or contribution. If the results from his department are not satisfactory, he can easily say; 'I did what you told me. If I had been allowed to make my own decision this would not have happened. The results would have been as planned.'

In short, the chief executive should advise, counsel, support, but not interfere with what an executive does within his own department provided that it is does not conflict with agreed operational plans.

If the chief executive does not feel he can leave it to the executive to make his own decisions, he needs to consider very carefully why he feels that way. If it is because of nagging doubts about the man's ability, without any real evidence, then the more the man is left to do his own job his own way the sooner will the chief executive really know what his abilities are. And if the executive has, in objective terms, a record of bad decisions leading to unsatisfactory performance, he should be replaced.

Chief executive as long-stop

What has been said in the previous section applies particularly when the company is engaged in critical negotiating, e.g. when there is a labour dispute. The chief executive must very firmly resist any temptation to step in and deal with the situation himself. One important reason for this is that it is often difficult in the heat of negotiations to perceive all the implications of a given proposal or suggested compromise. If the chief executive is there himself it may be difficult for him, as top man, to appear to prevaricate and he may feel a strong emotional pressure to make a decision on the spot. His subordinate in the same position has no such difficulty because he has the ready excuse that he must consult with the chief executive. This gives an opportunity for a cooler appraisal and a more deeply considered response than would otherwise have been possible.

Secondly, it is often tactically sound in any negotiation for the executive directly involved to take a relatively inflexible stance. He can do this in the confident knowledge that, if his inflexibility leads to a confrontation, there is a line of appeal to the chief executive that will enable the situation to be defused. This is particularly useful when the

108

issues are complex and where a wrong decision may have far-reaching consequences.

Recently, a colleague of considerable experience asked me what I thought was the main role of a chief executive. I gave some of the answers that I have put in this book; he then told me that he had asked some of his subordinates the same question and they saw the main role as 'getting done for them those things that they do not have the authority to get done themselves'.

I found that an interesting concept, because it reverses the view of the chief executive as one who plans and controls the work of his subordinates. And yet it is a valid viewpoint because it is also part of a chief executive's job to deal with those matters that prevent any of his subordinates doing their own jobs successfully and in their eyes he will be judged on how well he does this. It also gives an indication of the relationships in the company concerned because it implies consultation, a common purpose, action-orientated management and mutual trust and respect. It is a far cry from one executive I remember who dismissed one of his subordinates with the words: 'Don't come to me with your problems. I have got enough problems of my own.'

Trades unions

As far as relationships with trades unions are concerned the same principles apply. Trades union officials want their voices to be heard but they do not want to take over the management role. If there is a management vacuum, or management weakness, they will be forced to encroach upon what should be a management prerogative. But most trades union officials are concerned for the security and welfare of the members they represent. They want the enterprise to be well run and successful, and they know that managers must have freedom to manage. On the other hand, they are there to get the best for their members and, as in any other bargaining situation, they will usually start by asking for rather more than they expect to get. If the bargaining on the other side is not equally competent and equally positive, then management powers will be eroded.

In the course of my experience as a management consultant I have been in a number of companies where management seemed to have almost lost control. In some cases, quite outrageous practices had come into being — slow work pace, restrictive practices, disregard for normal shop-floor discipline, over-manning of machines. When asked about this management would say: 'We can't do anything about it. The unions are too strong. We can't afford a strike.' These statements at the time they were made were probably correct. The intrusion upon management authority had become a practice to such an extent that it was a 'right'. But it can be overcome. In many situations I have seen new managers take over and, by exercising positive leadership, reverse the adverse trend and create once more a positive management climate.

In one case the works manager, a man whose forceful manner concealed a timorous soul, had conceded many of the prerogatives of management to shop-floor representatives. He was convinced, and had succeeded in convincing his colleagues, that not to do so would invite major disruptions of production. In private, he fulminated against what he o be considered to be the effrontery of his workforce, but he always backed down when there was a risk of confrontation.

The work in the factory was mainly semi-skilled and un-skilled, but over the years a multiplicity of different hourly wage rates had crept in. By custom and practice, the more senior men were given the higher-rated jobs. Because absenteeism was relatively high (in itself a commentary on the state of morale), jobs were allocated daily and they were allocated by the men's own representatives, not by management. Every day, the first half-hour or so was lost, waiting for late-comers to arrive and then allocating men to their jobs. It had become something of a point of honour for every workman not to allow anyone with lower seniority to do a higher-valued job. Subtle variations on the definition of seniority were debated with doctrinal fervour, and disputes were frequent.

The works manager was certain that *they* would never let him change the situation and at the same time was deeply frustrated by it and also by the many other manifestations of the lack of management control that permeated the company. All of this he ascribed to *their* intransigence.

Then the works manager died of a heart attack (and one wonders how much the frustrations of his working days contributed to this). He was replaced by his deputy, a very different type of man. Although outwardly not as forceful as his predecessor, he had always been itching to get his hands on the reins and assert management's right to take effective control.

He immediately announced proposals to consolidate all hourly rates into three grades and to assign operatives to one of the three grades on a regular basis. The daily job allocations were stopped. The only concession made was that long-service employees were initially given the highest-rated jobs, provided they could perform them effectively. But he made it clear that from that day onwards, promotion to higher rates would be on merit.

All the managers expected a walkout and a hard-fought battle and most of them thought that at the end of it they would be lucky to re-establish more than a very small part of their lost authority.

Inevitably, the abruptness with which the proposals for the changes were introduced led to a dispute. But, in fact, it was a sham fight. Whilst the workers' representatives felt that they had to show that they were not prepared to allow themselves to be trampled on, privately they said to the new works manager at the very start of the conflict: 'We were sick and tired of doing your job for you and not getting any credit for it from our own people. At last, management is trying to do its own job.'

The new arrangements were soon accepted as were a number of other steps designed to improve the efficiency of the business. The company's performance had suffered for years because management wrongly believed they knew what their employees wanted and how they would react to changes. One explanation I was given of the men's real attitudes was that they had sensed the weaknesses behind the bombastic exterior of the old works manager and could not resist the temptation to show him they were not going to be intimidated.

Whatever the trades union organisation, whatever the attitudes of its members, confident and decisive management, practising genuine consultation, and always guarding management's right to make the final decision, will usually secure good industrial relations.

Professional competence

One last point needs to be made — a professional management climate can itself be a strong motivating force. People expect competent leadership, will readily identify it and will respond when they believe it to be present. I have seen this happen so often. A new manager is appointed and during his first few encounters with his subordinates, they can be seen to be holding back and trying to find out what sort of man he is and to judge how they should react to him. If he makes what they feel to be misjudgements or shows any lack of confidence in that early period he will find it very difficult to get their support and may never succeed in overcoming such an initial setback.

One newly appointed sales director in a company selling commercial vehicle equipment decided to spend a few days with each member of his sales force in order to find out how the business operated in the field, and to get to know each man better. In his anxiety to take positive control of the situation he insisted that one of the salesmen should take him on a cold sales call. He even nominated the prospect. The salesman was much against this because he said that there were no opportunities on his territory that he had not already approached and therefore the cold call would be worthless. The sales director insisted and the call was made. The prospect listened with courtesy to the salesman's presentation and at the end he said: 'I find your pitch very interesting but unfortunately we have no vehicles of our own as all our distribution is subcontracted? That was the end of the discussion. The salesman thought correctly that the sales director had made a fool of himself by forcing such an interview before he fully understood the market situation. The story became known and made the employees start to look for, and find, other signs of a less-than-sure touch, as a result of which the sales director's standing was considerably undermined and he eventually failed to hold down his appointment.

If on the other hand a newly appointed manager makes a constructive contribution early on, which shows that he obviously understands the company's situation and has useful ideas, then there is a perceptible feeling in his department of everyone drawing together to support him. Professional competence, therefore, is in itself an important element of management style.

8 Relationship with the Board

If all the members of the board of a company, apart from the chief executive, are non-executive directors, then his relationship with them can be reasonably straightforward. He proposes policies and actions to be taken and reports progress against approved company objectives. They approve or reject the former and query and investigate the latter. They also retain, reward or replace the chief executive, depending on how they judge his performance. In such a situation he is the sole channel of communication between the executive team and the board; the board has to rely on him for receiving information and ideas from within the company and for being briefed on matters that require policy decisions.

In the case of companies where other executives are members of the board, the situation is much more complex. Each one of such executive directors plays two quite distinct roles. As an executive working within the management structure he is responsible to the chief executive for his performance and has the duty to advise him on all pertinent management matters. As a director he participates in discussions on policy with exactly the same rights and responsibilities as every other director, including the chief executive.

The danger of damaging conflicts arising is quite apparent. If a director with functional responsibilities does not get his way at management level on an issue he considers important, he may try to get a decision reversed at a board meeting and, perhaps, get his chief executive overruled. True, only rarely will an executive think it politic to raise such a matter directly, unless the man is a fool. More often he may find himself in a delicate situation not of his own choosing. A sensitive topic may emerge at a board meeting without any prompting from the executive concerned. One of the non-executive directors may perhaps ask questions that reflect doubts about the wisdom of a particular decision. Or the executive concerned may be criticised for doing something he had originally opposed at the management committee. He has then the choice of either defending a decision with which he disagrees, or airing management disagreements at the board meeting.

The problem is obviously not an easy one to solve. In many companies it has been overcome by blurring the distinction between functions of the board and the management group, i.e. the chairman of the board becoming effectively a part-time chief executive, whilst the nominal chief executive acts as an operational manager dealing with day-to-day problems, without any real authority in strategic matters. In other companies the chief executive's standing or authority is so strong that none of the executive directors would even consider opposing him at the board table. This may appear to be quite a satisfactory situation as long as things do not go badly wrong with a company. If they do, then the other executive directors may be plausibly accused of failing in their responsibilities to the shareholders.

Difficulties and complications of working with a board may result from a variety of other structures that a chief executive will encounter in the course of his career. He may, for instance, become the head of a company which is a subsidiary of a major concern and his co-directors on the board may be important executives elsewhere in the same group. Little imagination is required to think of the type of problems this situation could create.

In all cases where there is a board with executive and non-executive members, the chief executive must make it clear to his colleagues what his views are about the dividing line between management and policy decisions. In other words, which matters should be decided by the chief executive after discussion with his management team and presented to the board as their considered opinion and which are matters of general policy where board discussions should not be inhibited by group loyalties. Of course, any executive director who feels strongly that a particular topic should be discussed at a board meeting has the right and the duty to raise it. But as has already been said, this should be done only after due thought and consideration, and the more carefully the chief executive has clarified his views to his subordinates the less will there be a need for such a challenge in the boardroom.

Policy versus management matters

The chief executive should also discuss with the chairman of the board which matters are appropriate for board debate and which concern management and should be referred to him for decision.

It is true that often the boundary between policy and management matters will be a vague one. But the general principles should be obvious. The chief executive is accountable to the board for the profitable operation of the business, within the framework of policies approved by the board. In order to carry out his job he must be able to make a wide range of decisions on his own authority. These will include, for example, decisions on the management structure and the selection and appointment of executives, decisions on tactical marketing and product policies, decisions on pricing, selection of plant, wage and salary policies. Other matters that are part of the continuous examination of the company's development have such far-reaching consequences that they must be considered as being policy matters and hence require boad approval. Decisions on company objectives, general marketing policies and significant capital expenditure, for instance, can cumulatively alter the fundamental nature of the business. There are other items which cannot be generally said to be either the responsibility of the chief executive or matters for board decision, because so much depends upon the significance of the decisions to that particular company in its own circumstances. But it is important for the chief executive to have the freedom of decision that he feels necessary in his own business context.

The crucial point is that a company cannot be managed from the boardroom, neither can it be managed effectively if the chief executive feels that his authority will be constantly overridden by the board. Yet every director is responsible to the shareholders for the profitable operation of the company. There is a genuine contradiction here and this poses a dilemma which requires that pains be taken to mitigate it. The chief executive must first be sure that he knows what authority he needs to do his job effectively and then try to ensure that he has it. His chairman may well disagree with his assessment and there may have to be discussions and compromises. But, in the end, there needs to be an explicit agreement on the method of working of, and the relationship between, the chief executive and the board of directors. Otherwise there will be unprofitable conflict and inadequate concentration on the needs of day-to-day management.

Non-executive directors

Non-executive directors sit on company boards for a variety of reasons, good and bad. Some are appointed because they have a broad range of relevant business experience and can bring to bear a detached judgement on the company's affairs, which it is not always possible to get from within the business. Others may have special expertise in a field of activity important to the company.

Far too many non-executive directors, however, are representatives of organisations with business relations with the company, e.g. its bankers, insurers, lawyers, consultants, etc. It has always seemed to me that such appointments are of dubious value, because these people have an interest in preserving their business relations with the company and would therefore not want to fall out with whoever can ensure that they continue. They are, therefore, unlikely to be out-spoken critics of the management of the business.

On the whole I believe that the board of a company should in the main be composed of non-executive directors without business links with the company, and that the only insiders should be the chairman and the chief executive and, possibly, the chief executive's designated successor, if such succession has been established. The reasons for this attitude have already been given: an executive director is often placed in the impossible position of having to perform a balancing act between his responsibilities to the shareholders and those to his colleagues, and also between his departmental interests and the interests of the company as a whole.

A board dominated by outsiders has other problems, but at least the responsibilities of the directors are straightforward. They are appointed to represent the shareholders' interests. As responsible businessmen they will also take into account the interests of the employees, public policies, ethical and moral constraints and other influences on the company's behaviour; but these will be considered to the extent that they bear on their primary responsibility.

The major problem of a board so composed is that the non-executive directors can spend at most a few days, and perhaps only a few hours, each month on the company's affairs. This means that the quality of their contribution will be to a large extent conditioned by the quality of information provided by the company. It is the chief executive's responsibility to oversee the preparation of this information. It is very tempting for him to arrange it in such a way that it will 'tell them what will make them happy'. He can do that by emphasising some aspects in his report or presentation and deal only cursorily with others. With his superior detailed knowledge of the company's affairs he may try, and be able, to blind the board to the true situation. It depends on the experience and shrewdness of the members of the board whether he can get away with it.

The excuse sometimes given for making a biased presentation is that the non-executive directors must be prevented from making foolish decisions. The inference is that they are inadequate. It is easy to argue this way. But could the real reason not be that the chief executive is acting that way to safeguard his own position or to get his policies accepted in defiance of the facts? If he is ever tempted to present to the board information that glosses over the company's problems and presents all trends in the most favourable light, he had better consider what will happen when the small cloud on the horizon has turned into a force eight gale.

A great deal of boardroom discussion may frequently be irrelevant or superficial, but from time to time a view will be expressed that should make the chief executive stop and think about some aspect of company business. Perhaps it will cast doubt on some cherished project, or point to the possibility of developing the business in a new direction. In any case directors who are outsiders not beholden to anyone in the company for their presence at the boardroom table deserve to have their views listened to with respect.

My advice to any chief executive would be to try to press for a board composed mainly of non-executive directors and, if possible, to avoid having to have his subordinates on the board. If this is not possible, then he must work out very carefully with his chairman the dividing line between his authority as chief executive and the policy-making authority of the board. He must then ensure the distinction is clearly understood by all concerned.

9 *Company Image*

Most people know very little about the companies they
buy from or invest in, or even those to which they give credit.
Even employees' knowledge of the companies for which they
work may well be limited to a single function or department.

More important, what people believe about a company is
often not based on the reality of the situation, but on an
image of the company that is quite likely not to reflect its
true nature. This image is very important. It has a strong
influence on decisions to buy the company's products, to
use its services, to invest in it, to work for it, or to lend it
money. Within the company, it helps to decide whether it is
felt to be a good one to work for.

In all these aspects, which have a strong bearing on the
company's long-term performance, the image is more
important than the reality; a company will be judged not
by what it is, but by what it appears to be.

I am not suggesting that the image can be entirely divorced
from reality. Real events will obviously have an influence on
the image, but the interpretation put on those events is
often conditioned by preconceived ideas about what the
company is and what it is trying to do. A company can do
things that are fair and even generous and yet have a

reputation for harshness and lack of humanity. This was true, for example, in the case of GEC in the UK when it acquired the AEI company. There were an appreciable number of redundancies but the treatment of those made redundant was generous, and the sums paid to them were considerably above the legal requirement. Yet the image of GEC at that time was of a predator cruelly dismembering the inoffensive dinosaur that had been AEI.

The reverse can happen as it did in the case of Slater Walker. The company created an image of great financial astuteness which allowed it to be valued in market capitalisation terms out of all proportion to its true worth. In parallel, a number of inexperienced, personable young men were allowed to flourish in the aura of the same company, share the power of its reputation, and themselves amass paper empires, in most cases on completely inadequate foundations, until reality dealt them their overdue come-uppance.

On the whole, I believe that real merit will emerge in the end, but I believe that the right image can vastly speed the process and a wrong one can certainly hinder it. I regard it, therefore, as a necessary condition for successful management that a company should make a conscious effort to develop the right image both to the outside world and to its own employees.

Internal image

Within a company, an image of integrity, competence and purpose can create a spirit that generates willing support for company policies. The image of what a company is and what its strengths and weaknesses are can also have a powerful influence on executives' decisions about what a company should do in the future. It is very important that what executives believe to be true about their company does in fact bear some relationship to the reality of the situation, because the wrong image of the sources of the company's strengths can lead to mistaken policies.

In any established firm one finds a corpus of folklore about its past, its strengths and its weaknesses. Long-service employees retail it, wistfully remembering the company's buccaneering days or the time they helped with the venture that started its growth or became the success story of its history. Of course, these stories are often regarded as the meanderings of old fogies, who hark back to the good old days when they were part of the firm's elite. But it is surprising how often one finds a new generation of executives accepting legends as history. This does not usually do much harm. On the contrary, sometimes it may help to make an *esprit de corps* not unlike the stories of past exploits in regimental histories.

It is only when such folklore influences decisions that there is trouble. In a crisis situation (and crises are a frequent occurence, although their scale varies), there is then a tendency to return to what are believed to be the old verities. 'This company has become what it is', said the chief executive to his assembled production executives, 'because it was the first to bring mass-production methods to what was then regarded as a craft industry. Others have followed our example, but we have always managed to keep one step ahead. Today this is no longer true. We have to regain this lead and I fully intend that we shall. This is where you gentlemen come in. I want to mount a cost-reduction exercise. . . .'

The firm went on declining steadily until its fortunes were reversed after a new chief executive took over. He realised that the problem was that changing market conditions had made the company's products out-of-date, and that higher productivity, however desirable in itself, was not the way out. Unencumbered by the false image of its past he saw that the firm's salvation lay in redesigning its products to suit modern tastes.

Many companies have such false ideas about the source of their strengths that do not do much harm unless they make decisions based on them.

Emphasis on strengths and principles

As far as its internal image is concerned, a company needs to decide what strengths are really important to it, and what principles should guide business decision-making, and then set about consciously to promulgate belief and support for those strengths and principles. Naturally, to create the image without the reality would be a meaningless or counter-productive gesture, but provided the intention exists, the creation of the image can often help the reality.

For example, if a company believes that a reputation for product reliability is an essential element in its marketing strategy then it needs to communicate to all employees the fact that the company will stand or fall by the reliability of its products, and that its products are the best on the market. This will help to persuade people to stop and think before doing slipshod work, or letting a suspect component be used in a product, or passing a borderline unit at final inspection or test. Thereby they will actually sustain the situation suggested by the image.

In other fields, employees may be surprisingly unaware of what their company represents and this may be due to management reticence. I have known companies that are constantly under pressure to increase rates of pay despite the fact that they are paying far above the typical rates of pay for similar work in the same areas. They have failed to convince their employees that they are doing very well indeed by comparison with the market in general. People do not automatically recognise that they are well paid and work under good conditions. They need to be told and reminded. Just as it is necessary to use a sales force to remind customers of the benefits the company offers them compared with competitors, so there is a need to remind employees of what the company is to them (by implication compared with the alternatives).

The first step in doing this is to decide what the company wants to communicate. The basic rule is that a few ideas should be selected which encapsulate the policies of the company and its views on the things necessary to improve performance. Every available channel of communication should be used consistently to convey the intended message.

For instance, a company may decide to enter certain overseas markets. It knows that because these markets are remote from its home base, and its own reputation is not established there, that product quality and reliability will be even more important than in the existing markets. It knows that it will be essential to gain an early reputation for reliability of delivery promises and security of supply, and it knows that the products will have to be tailored closely to satisfy local market needs.

It then sets about deliberately creating within the company an awareness of customer needs and attitudes by constantly emphasising the importance of providing the right products at the right time and of the right quality. All employees are informed by means of the company newspaper or other written media and consultative councils are used to discuss the needs of the situation. Managers set up project groups to deal with specific aspects, and treat communication as part of the groups' task. And so it goes on, until every employee is aware of what has to be done and starts to regard the company as one with a special interest in looking after the needs of its overseas market. The image slowly becomes a reality. It will not happen overnight and a single-shot campaign will fail utterly. What is needed is a consistent projection of objectives for as long as these hold good.

None of this will happen unless the chief executive puts his whole weight behind it. If he does not create the image he wants, no one else will do it for him. Other people can help but, within the company, he alone can really determine what is to be achieved.

In Chapter 4, I referred to the need for the chief executive to get around his organisation and communicate informally with employees on all sites. One objective of that process is to help create the company image that he wants by putting across his policies and ideas to the people he meets.

It is also important for all executives to convey a feeling of success and confidence. At times they may not feel at all successful or confident; they will be beset with problems, feel under stress, and perhaps be depressed because plans are not working out as hoped; but whatever the circumstances, it is wrong to let them influence the image presented to other employees. This starts with the chief executive. After all, if the chief executive inadvertently gives the impression that he feels dispirited, what else can his subordinates feel other than that things are going seriously wrong. Staying cool and confident under pressure may be difficult but it is very necessary.

External image

The external image of a company will play a large part in deciding what marketing policies it can successfully adopt. A company which has created an image of itself as a producer of high-quality goods can charge high prices and achieve above-average margins for its products. It cannot go for a mass market without putting its existing image at risk. Similarly, if the company has established its market position on the basis of low prices and value for money, it may be precluded from the quality market, regardless of how good a product it develops, simply because prospective purchasers will not accept that it has the capability of producing such products. Whatever the reality of the situation, its existing image will determine the market segments it can successfully enter. The image, not reality, will control the situation.

This is not to suggest that a company can never change its marketing posture; but it cannot do so without consciously and deliberately first changing its image.

There are many themes on which a company's image can be built. I have mentioned product reliability, quality and value for money; but there are other possibilities, such as technical support for customers, capability of producing special design solutions for customers, good after-sales service, and many more.

As in the case of the internal image, the first step is for the company to decide what image it wants to project. This, in turn, is decided by its marketing policies and, particularly, the extent to which it wishes to change its market position.

There is a large range of possible ways of creating an effective external image. Among these are the explicit instruments of image-building: advertisements, house style, PR activities.

Advertisements are such a routine part of the sales and marketing function that they are hardly likely to be over-looked as a means of creating a satisfactory external image;

but often advertising policy is decided in the marketing department on a product basis, and not as part of an integrated image-building plan. This is a mistaken approach. Advertising is more effective if it is reinforced by a consistent presentation of the true character of the company.

House style

A house style for all the company's internal and external communication can be a very effective aid to image-building. It can be used to create a specific feeling about the company. In a financial institution it might be used to convey a rather solid, slightly old-fashioned feeling. In another business it might be designed to convey technological strengths, or a bright modern image.

To develop a successful house style always needs good professional help and careful briefing. The only way to choose professionals for the purpose is to examine work that has been done for other companies in allied fields and then choose the designer whose work seems to be the most satisfactory. It is very necessary to brief the designer adequately about *what* the company wishes to convey, but it is usually a mistake to try to tell him *how* it should be conveyed. If he knows his job he will want to do it his way. If he adjusts the design to suit the opinions of the chief executive or, worse still, a committee of directors, the compromise is unlikely to be successful. It is better to brief him and then to accept or reject his work in its entirety.

The house style, once adopted, is used on every communication issued by the company: brochures, instruction manuals, letter headings, invoices, etc. It is used, where appropriate, on product labels and in product design. It is used on the company's vehicles, buildings, exhibition stands and anywhere else that the company name appears.

Projecting the image

The establishment of effective PR is also a necessary management task. Journalists are generally hungry for information; a company that takes the trouble to find out what kind of information is useful to them and sets out to present it in a suitable form will find no difficulty in getting its name in print regularly. It is usually helpful to employ an agent to process the material, to maintain the contact with the journalists and, even more important, to decide which kinds of journal are most relevant to the company's intentions. Most directors like to see their company mentioned in papers they read regularly; but it may be that PR activities should be directed almost entirely towards trade papers or the technical press. As in most things it is necessary to think through the objectives and plan the activities to achieve specific targets and results.

Apart from the overt image creation, there is the matter of training all the company's staff who have contact with the outside world, such as telephonists, receptionists, drivers, stores personnel, credit controllers, etc., to express a feeling of competence, integrity and concern for customers' interests. This includes, where appropriate: clean and tidy appearance, always being on time for appointments, returning a customer's telephone call when promised. It means being cheerfully responsive even when a customer is being unreasonable. Such attitudes do not come naturally; they do entail training and monitoring.

The chief executive has a vital role to play in deciding the kind of image he wishes his company to have in its market, to the financial world and to the general public; but it is not quite so essential that he should play as large a personal role in actually creating the image as it is within the company. It is much more open to him to use professionals to do the job of actually putting the image across. His job is to make sure that he knows what he wants to get across and that all the professionals in their various fields present a consistent picture. He must make sure that the advertising agents, PR consultants, the company's own sales force and all internal departments of the company that have any contact with the outside world are properly briefed to present a consistent picture.

Where outside specialists are used, it is not their job to decide what image the company should create; it is merely their job to provide the means of communication.

It is sometimes felt that, because a man has considerable experience in a particular field, he does not need to be briefed, that he must have 'been there before'. This is just not true. The first requirement is for the chief executive to share with his chosen adviser all the knowledge that only he can provide. This means an extensive and detailed brief on the general background of the situation, and on the specific points on which the expert's services are sought.

The need for this was exemplified to me once in the case of a company that hired a designer to update its house style. The designer was a man of considerable reputation, and his previous clients all thought very highly of his work. Because they knew he had done similar jobs very effectively in other companies, the directors assumed that he would be able to decide for himself the kind of image that needed to be presented. Actually, his real expertise lay in being able to make vivid visual shorthand statements, but he needed considerable guidance as to what they should convey. He was invited to attend a meeting with the directors of the company and was given an outline of the job. He then promised to produce tentative proposals within a few weeks. When these were presented at a subsequent meeting, there was universal dismay around the table, and the project was nearly terminated there and then. The directors had a quite specific view of their company and the kind of image they thought it should present. Perhaps there is fine distinction between a 'progressive' and an 'aggressive' image, but they felt that the designer had stepped over the line from one to the other. The project was brought back on the rails again by a thorough briefing session. At the end of it the designer appreciated what the directors wanted and they understood very much better what a designer could do and what his limitations were.

Exactly the same principles apply to the briefing of advertising agents. Left to their own devices, they will be full of ideas; but there is no reason why they should have any knowledge of what the company really wants to communicate unless they are deliberately and carefully briefed. They represent an expert channel of communication, but no more than that. If the chief executive leaves a void by failing to brief them fully,

they will be only too willing to assume that they know what
the company wants communicated; but their assumptions may
well be founded upon erroneous views of what the company
is really trying to do.

Image and reality

I have said earlier in this chapter that, in some aspects, the
business image a company creates may be more important
than the reality. This may give the impression that I am
advocating the creation of a false picture of the company, but
that is certainly not my intention. I suggested that it is good
for a company to present an image that makes it seem larger,
more successful and more effective than perhaps could be
justified by a coldly objective look at the facts, and I would
regard that as entirely legitimate. But there is great danger
in trying to create an image which is at odds with reality.
Those who know better will mock the company or the
executive concerned. From that will follow a slow spread of
disbelief even of those factors that are true and favourable. An
image must be firmly rooted in reality, even if a little poetic
licence is used in its presentation.

The need is, therefore, first to decide the company's
policies then to decide what concepts need to be conveyed
to the company's employees and to the outside world in order
to enhance the effectiveness of the chosen policies; then, with
those very much in mind, to use all the available forms of
communication to get the message across.

The chief executive's job is to make sure that he approves
the image that is being created and to monitor the success of
the operation.

10 Product Renewal

The concept of product life cycles is well established. All successful products go through a cycle of introduction, growth, maturity and eventual decline. The length of the life cycle varies tremendously, from possibly a few weeks in the case of a new pop record or the latest dress style, to many years for an item of industrial plant. But decline they all do, and if a company is to stay afloat it must ensure that new products are constantly passing through the various design stages and are being brought to the market at the right time.

The choice of the right products is quite fundamental to a company's long-term prospects. It may take time before the correctness or otherwise of a decision emerges. The time scale will vary depending very much on the company's product development period. The longer that period the more important it is that the original decision is right. Other factors will arise out of the nature of the business in which the company is involved. If a company is introducing whole ranges of new products, providing the majority are successful, a few failures will not matter very much. If, on the other hand, a company is relying on a few main product lines, as, for example, in the automobile industry, then a bad judgement can be disastrous.

Role of the specialist

In technically-orientated companies, product development is often left to the engineering department. Engineers, however, tend to get excited by interesting engineering solutions and technical excellence rather than by marketability, and the shelves of warehouses are littered with products which have everything going for them, except the desire on the part of their customers to buy them.

Engineers are far from being the only culprits, and it could be just as harmful to depend too much on marketing specialists for new product definition. They may have a very sound view of the current market position. They know what customers are buying and are knowledgeable about market trends, but they may not be aware of the potential effect of new technological developments on providing alternative means of satisfying customers' needs. Their very awareness of what is being offered by competitors may lead them to adopt a 'me too' attitude to new product development. They also tend to propose specifications for new products with an ideal mix of features and price that is unachievable. They then can excuse the weaknesses of their performance by pointing to the omission of essential features or to the high price of the product.

A similar story can be told of production engineers, manufacturing managers, cost accountants, etc. They will all have views about what attributes a new product range should have. And all of these should be taken into account when the decisions are being made. There is then the chance that the newly launched product will be well engineered, easy to manufacture, of adequate quality and performance and attractively priced.

In fact, new product definition and the control of development programmes are areas of activity that are quite often left to be dealt with by relatively junior functional specialists. The programmes they work out are then rubber-stamped by top management. This is, of course, quite wrong. Product renewal is a fundamental part of business strategy, and is one aspect of management which the chief executive must not just formally control, but where he must be deeply involved at every stage. It is a field in which it is painfully easy to be blinded by science, or by apparently factual analyses that are really based on flimsy assumptions; which long-term technical forecasts are not? There are few certainties and very large doses of judgement. Particularly in the case of complex products, it is a question of balancing the technological risks of innovation against the marketing risks of not being in the forefront of product design. A chief executive who leaves such judgement to other executives, particularly those who have a functional axe to grind, does so at his peril.

Development by committee

Even worse than leaving product renewal decisions to individual experts is for the chief executive to leave them to a committee. This is what happened in one company that felt it had to diversify its product range. A meeting was called of 'all interested parties', which meant in practice a number of marketing specialists, various members of the product development department, the financial controller and sundry senior executives in the manufacturing and servicing departments of the company.

At the first meeting the 'parameters' of suitable intended new product areas were drawn up. This was a lengthy process, because there were differing views about the company's existing fields of competence, and even when these were agreed, it was far from obvious which could be the best source of future growth. However, the meeting ploughed on and eventually recorded a series of 'parameters', i.e. requirements, which any new product range would have to satisfy.

At the next meeting, it was found that a number of the participants had had second thoughts about the conclusions of the first meeting and much of the ground was gone over again, until a new set of requirements was agreed. Then an attempt was made to think of products that would satisfy these requirements. It was then realised that the suitable fields of development had been so circumscribed in terms of the total market size, freedom from competition and the kind of skills to be employed, that they were searching for something that did not exist. When this dawned on the meeting, it was quickly decided that everyone should think about the matter further and that another meeting would be called in 4 weeks' time.

At that meeting the chairman decided that the problem would be dealt with in a different way, that there would be a brainstorming session to list all the possible fields the company might enter and then, by a process of elimination, they would create a shortlist for more detailed consideration. The brainstorming did not go very well at first, because the meeting was much too big and most of the people did not understand the process anyway and were therefore inclined to take each suggestion apart as soon as it was made, rather than wait to appraise it at a later stage. However, eventually a 3-page list was drawn up and the chairman decided that they should rank the ideas. There was a long discussion as to how this was to be done, and it took several meetings to carry out the ranking process.

It then turned out that, in the case of every suggestion on the top part of the list, the market was either too small to be of interest to the company, or there were so many people in it already that it would be very difficult to break into the market. This was hardly a very surprising discovery, for it is quite a normal situation. But it was a blow. The meetings eventually fizzled out and the company continued in its old ways. They had achieved nothing.

What had been obviously wrong was the assumption that such meetings could successfully do all the work necessary to decide on a course of action, whereas it is extremely rare that useful decisions can be taken at meetings unless careful preparatory work has been carried out. The main issues have to be analysed and, where possible, quantified, before a meeting takes place. If the participants had been properly briefed in this way, they would have avoided most of the problems encountered. They might even have reached some useful conclusions.

However, even if the meeting had been fully briefed and had reached worthwhile conclusions, it would have been up to the chief executive to make the final decision, for product renewal is too important and too fundamental to the future success of a business for him to forego his prerogative. It is also a typical high-risk area for a company — knowledge is limited, decisions must be based on personal judgement and there are always conflicting views.

Product range

The chief executive must decide, in accordance with the strategic plans of a business, the size of product range a company needs. This is determined by market requirements, by the amount of investment the company can affort to put into new products and by the management and financial resources available to sustain it. He must decide the direction of the company's product policy, choose which market need the company is best equipped to satisfy, which will provide the best potential return and how fast existing products need to be phased out and replaced. These are all judgemental decisions. Existing trends can be studied, competitors' activities appraised and market investigations undertaken. These will all provide data to help the chief executive to make up his mind; but in the end, however much data is accumulated, there will be no signpost. If there were, everyone would follow it, and it would pay to go in the contrary direction where competition would be less fierce, which is of course a very important point. A chief executive may well choose **deliberately** to take a different path from the one he perceives to be the main trend of the market, in order to generate a unique market position.

Summary

In product renewal, only four things are certain:
1   If product replacement does not keep pace with the decline of existing products, then the company itself will decline.

2   The right decisions are fundamental to the general
     strategy of the business.
3   Wrong decisions will take a long time to become
     apparent and may have serious consequences for the
     company.
4   The downside potential makes such decisons far too
     important to be left to the experts. The chief executive
     himself must make them.

11 Knowledge and Experience Required

Successful chief executives seem to emerge from any background of functional expertise, such as accounting, marketing or engineering. There is no single path to the top and it is, therefore, not easy to specify the knowledge and the experience that a chief executive should have. I am sure that, whatever I postulate, examples could be found to prove me wrong. I think, however, that there are some general fields in which a chief executive should be knowledgeable and without which knowledge he would be at a disadvantage compared with his competitors.

Apart from the ability to put a team together and inspire it to work effectively under him, I believe that the chief executive needs to excel in four main fields:

1   Skill in the analysis of company accounts and other numerical and financial data.
2   Knowledge of the strategic implications of marketing and the ability to take a marketing view of the company's strategy.
3   Ability to use expert advice and support, in a balanced fashion, in order to control those activities in which he is not personally proficient.
4   Sensitivity to other people's responses, which alone enables him to know when to act, when to wait, when to apply pressure, and when to let matters take their course.

136

Numerate skills

Any chief executive is presumably able to read a set of
company accounts and understand them, but complete
comprehension is another matter. Most adults can read,
but few can comprehend all the nuances of a technical or
legal treatise.

In any set of figures there are meanings at many levels: the
figures themselves, their trends, the ratios between them and
the trends of the ratios. Only a man who appreciates this will
read the figures in such a way as to grasp quickly how adverse
trends can be corrected and how performance can be improved.
It is one thing to know how the company's turnover and
profits have developed over the preceding five years and it is
another to read from the same figures the way in which the
employees' share of added value has changed during that
period, and why the change has taken place. A good chief
executive works through his figures, examining the key ratios
and trends, exploring the reasons for changes and (particularly
if he has a computer available) experiments by changing some
of the key ratios to find out how these would effect profitability and cash flow. As a result he may get a clear idea of
what steps need to be taken to improve his business or, at
least, he will know which areas of the company's activities
require investigation.

This does not require an accountant's brain; it does require
numerate skill, and for that reason I have reservations about
the long-standing British faith in administrators who are
educated in the humanities and who are without training in
handling technical information and numerical material. I
have more faith in American and European practice where
numeracy is regarded as an essential attribute of a potential
chief executive.

This is also important in handling non-financial data. As
I have indicated elsewhere, I do not believe that management
can ever be a scientific process, but I do believe that many
of the tools of scientific investigation can be applied to
management matters. This is particularly true of many
forms of statistical analysis. Obvious examples are the use of
statistical methods in the analysis of market research data,

the control of quality, the forecasting of short-term demand and the control of inventories. To some extent also the effective use of computers necessitates some understanding on the part of the chief executive of the basic principles involved.

What seems to be necessary is enough knowledge of statistical techniques to know what can be done with them and what their limitations are. This should be sufficient to allow the chief executive to employ them effectively and prevent his uncritical acceptance of statistical information supplied to him. Particularly, he must be aware of the various ways of checking the validity of any data supplied.

In this context I remember one engineering company with a quality problem in the assembly department. All the components used were being sampled regularly on a statistical plan in the machine shop, and all seemed to fall within the required limits; yet they did not go together as they should and selective assembly had become necessary, thus taking longer to do the job. All the tolerances were checked and rechecked and no obvious solution emerged until a young engineer in the design department asked to see the sampling reports which gave the critical dimensions of each sample taken. He took them home that evening and when he returned the following day he was able to say, without going to the machine shop and without measuring any of the items, that no sampling had been carried out, and that the inspector concerned had been filling in random information, presumably to avoid doing a rather monotonous job.

The obvious question was asked; 'How could he possibly know that the figures were not genuine without checking any of the items?'. The explanation was that he had selected one of the dimensions and plotted the alleged measurements on a graph which should have shown a recognisable normal distribution curve. What he had expected to find was that this had become distorted, perhaps through some machine fault. Instead, he found that the graph was incompatible with such a normal distribution curve. The shape of the curve proved that the data used was invalid.

I do not suggest that the chief executive should be a statistician, only that he should know of the statistical tools available and be skilled in the use of such data.

If I appear to be labouring this point it is because I have seen too many managers discuss projects and make decisions largely on a qualitative set of factors, whereas had they said at an early stage: 'How many?. How much? What is the trend? What are the confidence limits?', they might have come to a different decision.

Marketing knowledge

All really successful entrepreneurs have the art of getting inside a customer's mind, finding out the service that he really wants, and then setting out to provide just that. They do not think primarily in terms of selling a product or a service already available, or filling existing capacity, but in terms of satisfying needs.

They may not do this as part of an organised discipline. They do it because they have learnt by experience that the best way to generate business is to bend to the other man's needs rather than to cause him to bend to one's own needs. That, in a single sentence, is what I mean by a marketing attitude.

It comes instinctively to a chief executive who has successfully built his own business; it may not do so to one who has climbed to the top by being a first-class engineer, accountant or manager in an already established company, particularly if it is a large one.

The prevalent attitude there may well be that the company's market position is well established, its products in strong demand, and so what really matters is to hold down costs, improve design details, and sell hard against the competition. Unfortunately, such companies, like those in the once world-renowned British motorcycle industry, wither in the wind of aggressive, market-orientated competition.

Market orientation means organising the whole company, all departments, to seek out and satisfy customer needs. This includes product design and development, manufacturing, credit management, spares and servicing departments, as well as those normally associated with the marketing function.

If this is done skillfully, it will go a long way towards reducing the traditional rivalry between sales and manufacturing. If these two departments are working to achieve agreed marketing aims conflict is less likely to arise.

This does not mean that the company should attempt to satisfy every customer need. That would only create a proliferation of products and prevent the company producing any of them economically. What it does mean is to select those needs which the company intends to satisfy, and then gearing the business to achieve these aims and no other.

There will always be voices saying: 'If only we had another product to fill this or that niche in the market'. It takes a clear assessment of policy, and courage, to insist that only those customer needs which coincide with the company's marketing objectives will be fulfilled. But only by doing so can the company's resources be fully geared to satisfy customers in the most effective way.

It is important to be able to distinguish between what a customer says he wants and what his real needs are. Customers may not be clear about their needs, because normally they are only taking into account comparisons with products which already exist, and they may also be voicing traditional attitudes no longer truly valid. Customers' expressed opinions are often significantly more conservative than their actual behaviour. They frequently decry the need to make changes to established products, only to take them up eagerly once they appear on the market. It is often a matter of not wanting change but also of not wanting to be left behind. In discerning customer needs, it is, therefore, necessary to examine in some depth how the product is actually used and not rely too much on what the customer says about its use.

Customers may also mislead when they reject a product, because if they like the salesman they may not want to hurt his feelings, so they tell him what they think he wants to hear. Sometimes they criticise product features and claim that other products available to them are more satisfactory just as a means of bargaining for a lower price.

I remember once completely redesigning a product to meet a customer's stated requirements only to find at the end that he was really satisfied with the standard product, but

just had general reservations about the company's ability to
supply. His criticisms of the product were just a round-about
way of saying no. Fortunately the speed of the redesign
convinced him that his fears about the company were un-
founded and he did place an order for the standard product,
so the work was not entirely wasted.

What all this means is that the chief executive does need
to have contact with the decision-makers in his customer
companies and shrewdness in reading other people's minds.
He must also be very firm-minded about segmenting his
potential market and tackling one segment at a time. The
military maxim of applying maximum strength on a narrow
front is very relevant to marketing decisions and it is so easy
to become diverted.

Use of experts

It is neither possible for a chief executive to be an expert
in all the fields in which a company operates nor is it
important that he should be. It is not, for example, necessary
that he should be able to specify unaided the most effective
manufacturing processes for his company, the most suitable
plant, and matters of this kind. He must, however, be
capable of making informed judgements about whether or
not the performance in a given field is satisfactory when
compared with other companies operating in the same type
of business. This is much more important than knowing how
to improve the performance, for if he knows that it is not
satisfactory, he can always hire the necessary expertise to
get it right. The real danger arises when he uncritically accepts
the diagnosis of a problem and its solution as seen by an
expert in one field of knowledge. He may then find out too
late that he has accepted bad advice — not that the expert
was trying to mislead him, but because an expert viewpoint
is a specific one and, therefore, the picture he presents will
almost always be too limited and narrow to stand in its own
right. Looking at a problem in terms of his own expertise,
he may well ignore a great deal of relevant data if it happens
to fall outside his own field and will tend to give greater

prominence to those matters falling within it. It follows that if the picture he presents is adopted too readily, it may lead to unsatisfactory decisions being taken.

I am reminded of a factory where the final test arrangements needed to be reorganised because of the apparently serious congestion in that department. When the semi-skilled testers found any faulty products, they used to pass them on to fault-finders who specified what needed to be done and, in turn, passed them on to the repairers. Once the faults had been rectified, the products were returned to the test section. The varying build-up of products within this loop created constant log-jams and problems of space and movement. Therefore, a very able young materials-handling engineer was assigned to solve the problem. He accepted the challenge with confidence and soon designed an elaborate conveyor system to transport the products between the various sections and to hold the largest predicted number between the work stations.

The new system was installed at considerable expense. It was then found that the situation in the testing department was as bad as before, but for different reasons. In the old layout the main problems were the physical handling of the products and of having nowhere to put them whenever an excessive number accumulated. This had been solved, but the new conveyor system was an obstacle to people moving about, which proved a serious inconvenience. The worst result, however, was that the testers, fault-finders and repair men were separated by yards of conveyors and there was no longer any informal contact between them. Under the old system, if a repaired product came back to a tester and was found to be still faulty, he could immediately draw the fault-finder's attention to it. (This feedback was also important in developing the skills of the fault-finders.) With the new system, products sometimes had to be recycled repeatedly before the faults were finally eliminated and it soon became just as choked as previously.

When this happened, top management took a serious interest in the problem for the first time. They soon came to the conclusion that this was not a materials-handling problem at all, but one of job structuring. The testers were trained in fault-finding, the elaborate conveyor system was removed, and the repair men were placed in close proximity to the testers. Within a few weeks the log-jam disappeared. The young engineer was disillusioned, but it was not his fault. He had done an expert materials-handling job, trying to resolve what had proved to be the wrong problem.

An analogy to the use of expert advice is perhaps the taking of aerial photographs of a land area at different light frequencies, from infra-red to ultra-violet. If the photographs are placed side by side, they reveal the same main features and are self-evidently of the same location; but the detailed information they can provide is quite different. Photographs taken in the infra-red part of the spectrum can reveal temperature distribution, enable deductions to be made about the nature of the crops being grown and about the presence of certain industrial processes, etc., with an accuracy that could not have been achieved with photographs taken in the visible part of the spectrum. At other frequencies, other features would be revealed. If anyone looked at each of the photographs in isolation and tried to deduce the characteristics of the areas, he would be able to make some useful deductions, but much of the information would be difficult to interpret and some would be misleading. Only by considering all of them would he start to get a proper picture of the area.

Similarly, experts of different disciplines, looking at a company and trying to estimate its future performance, might come to differing and contradictory conclusions. An economist might examine the effect of general economic trends on the company's markets and assume that these would be the dominant factors; a marketing specialist might focus his attention on the strengths and weaknesses of its product range and on the points in their life cycle the products have reached, from which he might predict an outcome not in accord with general market trends; a financial analyst might concentrate on how effectively the company's physical assets had been used in the past and on its profit record, from which he might foresee a gloomy future because past performance had been inadequate, and he may be blind to the potential effect of new products about to be launched which could transform its prospects.

This is a very much simplified picture; it only illustrates that from the vantage point of their individual expertise, experts can draw different conclusions. Each of the specialist views does provide important insights; but each omits far more than it includes and what has been omitted may have more fundamental consequences than what has been included. In short, an expert evaluation of any situation can be of value provided that it is used in conjunction with other forms of expertise to arrive at a true synthesis. If taken in isolation, expert truths almost always mislead.

In any field in which he doubts his own expertise, a chief executive should make sure that he consults people with different disciplines, in trying to get a balanced viewpoint. This is particularly important if he is thinking of introducing a new manufacturing process, new control procedures, or a computer. (Systems analysts and programmers are notorious for taking a computer-based view, rather than a management one, and are generally far more anxious to show what their marvellous machines can do rather than to solve the existing management problem in the simplest possible way.)

External expert advice also needs to be handled with care. If experts are used for narrowly defined tasks, well and good. I am less sure that external advice can be of real value in solving a company's fundamental problems.

In my career as a management consultant I have usually found that when a company has severe problems, advice on how the organisation or management systems of the company can be changed is rarely effective in improving the situation. The reason for this is that the quality of the implementation of any policy tends to be considerably more important than the policy itself. Company success is achieved by doing relatively simple things, but doing them well. If a company has problems that justify the involvement of management consultants, it is very likely that the quality of management is deficient, or that there are weaknesses within the whole spectrum of management activities. It is hardly surprising, therefore, that in this situation, external advice rarely produces the desired effect. But, by contrast, the appointment of a new chief executive may often bring effective results given the right time scale.

Timing

A chief executive needs to have a good appreciation of the
time scale in which his decisions can become effective. This
is dependent upon a number of different factors. One of
these is the size of the business itself. A small business can
be made to react very quickly to changes in policy. In a
large business it is easy only to make and implement negative
decisions, e.g. to close a factory, reduce staff, or sell off
obsolete stocks. It is very much more difficult, and it takes
much longer, to implement creative decisions such as a
move into a new marketing territory, the development of
new products, or the introduction of new expertise into the
business. If a chief executive does not have a feel for such
a time scale he may easily over-react if the expected outcome of his decisions does not emerge as early as was
anticipated, and may create worse problems by such
impatience.

This is illustrated by the case of a subsidiary company
producing several disparate engineering products. It was
looked upon by the group who owned it as its main problem
child, and justifiably so. In the past years, the subsidiary had
suffered through a succession of changes at the top and
through a change in location. But it was now being hit very
hard because the product range it had relied upon to generate
over 40 per cent of its income was being sold to an industry
undergoing a world-wide contraction.

The only bright feature in the situation was the
company's technological expertise, and indeed in certain
fields its technical competence was unrivalled. There seemed
no way out but to use this to improve existing products and
develop new product ranges and in the meantime for the
company to draw in its horns. This strategy was indeed
adopted, albeit in a somewhat confused and half-hearted
manner. The only part of it that was energetically pursued
was the thorough examination of overhead expenses, which
were severely pruned, mainly through staff reductions in
most departments.

At group headquarters the moves were welcomed, but in
view of their past experience with this subsidiary, group

executives thought it necessary to send a steady stream of exhortations. When a year had gone and the financial returns indicated little improvement in the company's fortunes, the chief executive was called to headquarters and given to understand that their patience was near the end.

He returned to call a meeting of his main executives and told them in effect that 'something must be done, for they want to see action'. In a state of near-panic, they adopted the first 'solution' which came into their heads, and instructions went out to all departments to cut their staff again, with a minimum target of 10 per cent. The effect of this second wave of redundancies was deadly. Morale collapsed, the people who remained having lost all confidence in the firm's future. The brightest young engineers left of their own accord and the company's greatest asset, its technological know-how, was nearly destroyed. But they could show headquarters that they were 'doing something' about the situation.

In this case the real solution — the renewal of the product range — was bound to take an appreciable time to have any effect on the results and, clearly, tight overhead control was essential while this was taking place. But to concentrate on the palliatives instead of the cure, just because the effect was more immediate, is a typical but unfortunate response of some executives when they are under pressure.

One of the problems with counselling patience in achieving a reversal of a bad situation is that the financial press is full of success stories, and many of the whizz kids of the last 20 years achieved their success by their ability to produce profits out of situations in which the previous management had failed. The secret is, however, not difficult to find. Almost without exception, their solutions were negative ones. Close this, sell off that, merge these two units. Essentially they were operations to stop losses and, therefore, to allow the profits of the remaining viable parts of the business to emerge. There is nothing wrong with actions of that kind for short-term profit improvement, but they do nothing whatever for the long-term future of the businesses concerned; which is precisely why so few of the stock market meteors actually stay the course, and build successful long-term businesses. However, their reputations have created expectations which good managers, with long-term objectives in mind, may find it very hard to meet. A good chief executive knows this and expects progress, but not miracle cures.

He needs enough experience of human kind to know how to motivate people; to know when to praise, when to criticise, when to overlook, when to kick up hell, when to put on the pressure and when to relax and let things take their course. These skills must mainly be learnt through experience and cannot be formally taught; but a chief executive who tries consciously to put himself mentally in the position of his subordinates and understand their problem is more likely to do this successfully than one who is uniformly demanding. I am suggesting, in this context alone, that there is virtue in inconsistency. That may be taking things too far; but every Chapter 7, but it does not in fact do so. A response should always be flexed according to the circumstances. The consistency lies in deliberate assessment of the circumstances not in the uniformity of the response.

12 Snares and Delusions

The chief executive is subject to a number of occupational hazards. Other executives may also be exposed to them but they are relatively immune to infection, because there is always someone to tell them that their judgement is becoming clouded, their manner a little strange and that they might actually make an occasional mistake.

The chief executive has no such safeguards. If he chooses to try to walk on the water, he may find that no one tells him of the probable consequences until his hat is afloat. Perhaps every chief executive, like a mediaeval monarch, should have a court jester to remind him that he too is ignorant, prejudiced and fallible. That he may be taking things too far; but every chief executive needs at least one good right-hand man whom he absolutely trusts, and who is privileged to be frank and outspoken with him.

Delusions of grandeur

Anyone who has read this book so far is unlikely to be suffering from this particular problem, but as it is an insidious disease it needs mentioning. A chief executive may behave as if his position conferred not just responsibility and authority, but also special knowledge and superior awareness. To maintain his status and superiority he starts to behave in such a way that these are clearly sustained. He ensures that his office, his car, his general life style are clearly better than his subordinates — better in kind not just in degree. He is the king; they are the court and let no one forget it, least of all those outside the magic circle.

He may even come to believe his own PR and when that happens all hope is lost.

A chief executive who has had a period of success may come to believe that the success is his and his alone, and that he has a special right to it. If he is fortunate there have been enough failures along the way to prevent this view taking hold; but if he is singularly unlucky and goes on being successful, he may then take more and more risky decisions in the implicit belief that he is infallible, until the inevitable disaster strikes. I am not suggesting that such an executive would claim infallibility, but like a gambler on a winning streak who feels that it can go on for ever, he bets with ever-increasing stakes, so that when the odds finally turn, everything he has is at risk.

Focus on personal strengths

My own early experience was in manufacturing and, because for about 10 years I was mainly a manufacturing executive, I still feel at home in a factory. I know how a typical works manager, production controller, industrial engineer, or foreman, is likely to respond in any given situation. The chances are that I have been in that situation myself. If there are any problems causing any one of them concern, I feel, rightly or wrongly, that I can usually put my finger on the solution.

Also, I am in a strong position to criticise what is going on in a factory as I am able to assess productivity rates, plant utilisation, and the effectiveness of the engineering and control departments.

In the fields of financial control and marketing, I acquired knowledge later and, although I would regard myself as competent in these fields, my grasp of the detailed operations of such departments is very much more limited than in manufacturing. For example, I know what information I want from a management accounting system, but I certainly could not advise on the best internal procedures to produce it. Equally, I regard it as the chief executive's job to control the company's marketing strategy; but I would certainly require expert support for the preparation of a market research programme, an advertising campaign or a merchandising plan.

As a result, I am always tempted to become more closely involved with detailed decisions in a manufacturing area than in the other functions. This is because I feel that I can see so clearly what needs to be done, and how it can be brought about. In the other areas I am much less tempted to do so because I know that I could easily be wrong in my understanding of the details of the operations or the tactical situation and perhaps make a fool of myself.

As a result I find that I must make a conscious effort not to get involved in manufacturing, and not to give the manufacturing manager unsolicited helpful advice. After all, if he needs my advice all the time, he is the wrong man for the job.

Every chief executive has a similar problem. Each must have started his career with particular strengths and gathered specific skills along the way so that he will be able to contribute more strongly in some departments than others. A problem arises when a chief executive fails to recognise that there is one, and focuses too much of his attention into the area where he is most expert. This can do considerable damage to a business.

In every business, the different departments, treated in isolation, have conflicting interests. Manufacturing executives would like to have long production runs, a small range of standard products, heavy stocks to ensure continuity of output, and products designed primarily for ease of manufacture. Sales executives want a large product range to meet every possible customer need, large stocks of finished goods so that all products are available from stock, great flexibility of production so that sudden increases in demand can be met with immediate response, products with a better specification and lower price than their competitors'. The engineers tend to design products that are technically interesting and sophisticated but they are usually not very interested in designing down to a cost. They tend to put in features that *they* want rather than features that *customers* want and think of educating the customers to like the product rather than designing it so that it meets the customer's needs. Accountants want low inventories of both finished goods and materials, low manufacturing costs, high selling prices, and standard products because this makes it easy to institute effective costing systems.

There is not only a great deal of conflict between these requirements, but it is also evident that accepting any one in its entirety could be damaging to the company's interest. What is needed is the right balance to optimise performance, which is a matter of very fine judgement.

If the chief executive fails to throw off his early allegiance and allows his own functional interest to predominate, such a balance will not be achieved. I have encountered this situation in many companies and with many different dominant functional specialities. In one case, a sales director had been promoted to chief executive and the production department was in constant turmoil, changing priorities almost daily to react to the latest state of the order book. Up to a point responsiveness is fine, but not when it creates such inefficiency that margins are nullified, or when it so demoralises the manufacturing executives that only the most malleable and least effective remain. Domination by engineers has also broken many good companies, because they forget that they have to produce what the customer needs.

It is not possible to entirely avoid a tendency to see problems and situations in the terms of one's own expertise but it is very necessary for a chief executive to make a conscious and sustained effort to avoid doing so, and preserve the right balance between the various functional requirements.

Drugged by detail

In any business there is a constant stream of data demanding the chief executive's attention. He can either get involved himself, or delegate much of it to his subordinates. Some chief executives try to do far too much themselves. They do this either because they have insufficient trust in the competence of their subordinates (which is an indictment of themselves, because they are responsible for the quality of the team) or because they feel insecure if they do not know in detail what is going on in the business and fear that they are getting out of touch.

Business is stressful and a chief executive is vulnerable to the effects of stress. When a business has severe problems and the chief executive begins to realise that he is not able to resolve them, one typical response is for him to get even more involved in a set of routines that occupy his whole working day. Then he can say to himself in effect (although, of course, not explicitly): 'I would like to deal with that problem, but I am so busy that I just do not have time'.

The answer to this basic problem of getting too deeply involved in detail is to plan effectively and to deal with problems as soon as they emerge, as that alone makes delegation comfortable.

Any chief executive who finds himself getting too busy to deal with the unexpected event, or finds he has no time in his working day to sit back and contemplate his business situation, should regard this as a warning sign. In this situation, my advice would be that he should take a few weeks' holiday and, on his return, before he becomes immersed in the detail of business again, he should shut himself up with his immediate subordinates, and hammer out with them a plan to resolve the problems of the business and to delegate implementation so as to reduce his own personal workload.

Doing is all

The opposite problem is that posed by the chief executive who believes that every problem requires decisive action. Sometimes a problem needs just that, but sometimes the need is for slow deliberate step-by-step adjustment of a situation to achieve a desired effect. For instance, it may be decided to change a company's marketing posture. It may have built its business by making special products to customer orders, and the chief executive may have realised that although this was a good way of achieving an early market penetration, there is now a need to standardise the company's products and get the costs down in order to gain a larger market share. To make the change overnight would be a recipe for disaster because the company would lose the market it has long before the new market segment could be developed. Such a policy might also require the retraining of his staff, new marketing skills, new attitudes, etc., all of which will take time to accomplish.

The trouble is that an executive who is too action-orientated may be so impatient for results that he will become dissatisfied if the effects of decisions are not soon evident, and then will either try and push too fast and so directly generate unnecessary crises, or become so impatient that he makes new decisions which modify or cancel the previous ones before they have time to have their due effect.

Indeed, action may even be an essential comforter for some people. There are executives who feel they are not doing their jobs properly unless they are stirring things up. To them, doing is all. The patient wait to verify the effect of a change, the nursing of new procedures through the inevitable crisis of confidence and the fine tuning when weaknesses in the new procedures arise are not for them.

I knew a chief executive who had very many admirable attributes. He was hard-working and quick-witted, he had a superb feeling for market trends, shrewdness in negotiations, and a charm which was consciously used to make men and women agree to do what they had no intention of doing. He had undoubtedly the makings of a very successful businessman but for a peculiar restlessness that did not allow him to let things be.

One day he would declare the layout of the administration block to be inefficient and start playing musical chairs with the offices. Another day he would demand changes in the costing system, which had just been professionally recast (with his enthusiastic approval). Then he would suddenly change the firm's pricing policy which he himself had carefully enuniciated only a few months earlier. And so it went on . . . The staff lived in a state of constant upheaval and there was much grumbling and head shaking. Our chief executive, however, was never happier than when he saw that 'something is being done at last'. He seemed to resent the slowness with which carefully laid business plans fructified and to compensate for the tedious waiting for results by orgies of instant change. In the end, there was an exodus of exasperated executives, the stability of the firm was completely undermined and a collapse was only avoided by a takeover.

It is natural for a chief executive to be impatient for results. It is essential that he does not allow his impatience to override his judgement. It is also important for him to recognise that any rapid action is as likely to demoralise as it is to vitalise an executive team.

Search for order

Almost every management strength, taken to excess, leads to weakness. One of these is the search for system and order. It is so obviously undesirable to tackle too many problems at once that some chief executives seem to take the opposite approach and try to deal with one problem at a time. This sounds very fine in theory but, unfortunately, management problems do not come singly and it is always necessary to strike a balance between operating on too many fronts at the same time, and making too many tactical changes, and the opposite of concentrating activities in one sector and being too inflexible to other influences.

A good illustration is provided by the history of a company producing electronic equipment for professional and industrial use. Their profit margins were low and this seemed to be due to a combination of low productivity, over-elaborate product design and an over-aggressive pricing policy. The latter had resulted, however, in a substantial forward-order book and therefore the attention of all the managers was focused on getting more output. An improvement in productivity was achieved through an intensive programme of work study and with the help of the product development teams, who modified many of the items being produced in order to simplify manufacturing and assembly operations.

As the chief executive had given absolute priority to the improvement in output, the product development department had concentrated all their efforts on this task. The assumption had been that as soon as the output had risen to the desired level, they would resume their work on the development of new products. However, the improvement in output was short-lived, because when the products started to move through the factory in greater volume, stoppages through material shortages became increasingly frequent and it became obvious that there were serious weaknesses in the procurement system. These had been there all the time, but had been masked by the other causes of the inadequate rate of output.

Improving materials management then became the priority task. One method used was a rationalisation of components and the preferential use of a limited range of standard parts, which substantially reduced the number of different items required. This lightened the load on the materials management department and led not only to an improvement in the supply of materials, but also to a reduction in the company's inventory.

However, as this had once again necessitated modifying the products so that they would accept the standard components and parts, the development department and the drawing office had been busy designing and proving these modifications.

By the time everything had been put right, the forward-order book had evaporated because competitors had introduced a number of new products of improved design. The repeated diversion of attention from product development, because of the need to cope with its other problems, put the company's existence in jeopardy. It eventually recovered, but only after two very difficult years.

Another aspect of the search for order was referred to earlier — the concentration of management attention on producing an efficient administrative machine and having tightly controlled procedures for all aspects of the company's operations at the expense of innovation and enterprise. It is always true that new initiatives disturb the established situation and, because they give rise to a certain amount of uncertainty and entail a learning period, they make the company less efficient in the short term. For this reason a chief executive who is too much concerned with running an orderly business may well choke innovation at source, not intentionally, but because its first stirrings disturb his well ordered territory.

It is true to say, therefore, that order in management is important, but order alone can only help to run an efficient administrative machine and cannot actually make a company successful. To do that it is necessary to have flair, judgement and courage to take risks. The chief executive must know when to ignore the pundits and the prophets and follow his own lonely hunch.

The science of management

Management is not a science. Certain aspects of management are open to a scientific approach but that is an entirely different matter. In science, once one has established or observation or experimentation the basic laws affecting a given process, it is possible to say with certainty that a specific action will always lead to the same predictable outcome. This is not at all true of management. Management is not always tidy or logical. It cannot be so, because every aspect depends on a very complex interplay of individual human reactions.

One can obviously use general 'laws' which one knows from experience or study are generally applicable, but unlike scientific laws the relationship is rarely precise or certain. For instance, if a productivity bonus scheme is applied to a department previously on time-work, productivity will normally increase by at least a third. I know from experience that this happens, and the supposition is embedded in conventional management wisdom. But I also know that sometimes operatives refuse to work under bonus conditions or, once the scheme is installed, concentrate on finding loop-holes in it or pushing up the time standards rather than actually producing more.

The best I can say about my general 'law' is that it usually works. This is true of every aspect of management. A market

156

survey can be useful to provide information on what customers are currently buying and what they think about the products available and their attitudes to the suppliers concerned. It is also possible to ask questions that are intended to help formulate new product policy, but here the results are far less certain. The best that can be said is that a well researched product has a rather better chance of success than one that has not been thoroughly researched. But there are plenty of examples of product decisions founded on the best available marketing information miserably failing and, equally, products which could not be justified on the findings of market research being promoted with determination and becoming wildly successful. The Xerox process is one such example.

I do not wish to decry the efforts of all those who have fought so hard and for so long to wean management away from the 'rule of thumb' or the 'intuition is all' schools. All attempts to systematise and categorise knowledge in the management field need to be applauded. The increasing use of objective criteria and numerically defined data can be seen as a sign that the scientific attitude and approach is more prevalent today than ever before. But it is no use deluding oneself that because management is now increasingly numerate it is already a science.

Panaceas

Magic is in fashion. The spate of new religions and pseudo-religions that have emerged in the last 20 years or so confirms this. We have ancient gods from outer space, religions born of science fiction, mystery men from the east, to name just a few. Why should management be without its own magicians? The truth is that belief in magic is far from extinct. A few days ago an offering from a most reputable consultancy firm appeared on my desk and amongst other things I read with interest were the rhetorical questions:

> Are you taking management decisions without being certain of the outcome?

> Would you like to know in advance the effect of your
> decisions on your company's results?

There were more questions in the same vein and I was
intrigued and read on. It transpired that the firm was offering
a computer program which purported to provide a
generalised company financial model. This was the device
that was going to remove all uncertainty from management
decisions! What the brochure quite omitted to point out was
that the value of such a model was entirely dependent on the
validity of the assumptions, both general and particular,
upon which it was based and these were all matters of
judgement and considerable uncertainty. A claim that such
a model could remove uncertainty from management
decisions was obviously spurious.

The most disturbing feature of all was the possibility that
they actually believed what they had written. I could have
almost forgiven them if they had written it, tongue in cheek,
as a rather overstated sales promotion; but the thought that
someone offering advisory services to management really
believed that such a programme could give more than
marginal support to management decision-making was, to
say the least, puzzling.

Almost every management consultant is selling magic of
one kind or another. He is saying, in effect: 'You have a
problem which you are unable to solve; but I am initiated
into the mysteries, which enables me to solve it for you'.

The case of an ailing company with weak management will
illustrate the point. The main reason for their difficulties
was the failure to adjust their product policies to the
dramatic changes in their market. They were selling their
traditional products in ever-declining quantities and at
lower profit margins. There were a few promising new
products but they had never been properly promoted,
partly because the concentration on selling their old lines
left little resources for their exploitation. What the company
needed above all were clear and firm policies on new products
and markets and a determined excision of all unprofitable
activities. Nothing particularly clever or subtle was required,
just straightforward, good management.

158

Unfortunately the consultant who walked in just at the time the crisis peaked was an expert in method study and, having made a survey of the factory, recommended methods improvements and an incentive scheme in the toolroom. The ensuing assignment produced an appreciable increase in productivity and the identifiable savings per year more than offset the cost of the assignment; but the cost in time lost before the real problems of the company were dealt with was unquantifiable.

Was the consultant, who was an expert in method study and had come to sell his expertise, to blame? Or was it the fault of management who allowed him to sell them something of marginal benefit and to get distracted from the central issues of their business? It was, of course, management's fault. They had bought an assignment without having (or having had) investigated the real needs of the company and had taken the easy way out of accepting the first thing offered. They had passed part of their responsibility on to someone who was in no position to assume it and who was pursuing his own interests.

They did it because he was an expert. If someone within their own company had come forward with the same proposal they would have seen how preposterous it was. But because this man came under his magic cloak of expertise and because his fee was substantial they believed in what he had to sell.

It is curious to note that chief executives tend to be particularly susceptible to the influence of fashion in management. I have met chief executives propounding ideas that have been sold to them as the latest and greatest breakthrough. The managers in the departments concerned, however, regarded them as commonplace, as concepts they have been using in different forms for many years. But if the ideas have been sufficiently well dressed-up, they may find it impossible to convince their boss that all he had been sold was a fancy package. They may indeed decide that it is easier to pay lip service to the new wisdom, to placate its purveyor and to go on operating just as they had done before.

Buying expertise is a valid reason for using consultants,

provided that the company knows what it wants. This is particularly important in cases where new techniques are being introduced into the company. It means that the chief executive must make sure that he, or a member of his staff, finds out what can be expected from the technique and what are its limitations. It is his job to decide what kind of programme will improve the performance of his company, and to buy only expertise that will assist in implementing this programme.

Every new management technique has weaknesses and bad side-effects. No technique has universal application. No technique can actually solve any underlying business problems. They are all tools which can be well or badly used and, like most tools, if misused they can inflict injury on the user.

There are no panaceas. A man who sells his own expertise as if he is offering such a panacea is not to be trusted. The chief executive must make sure that he understands any new technique being offered before he accepts it and he must monitor its application in his business to satisfy himself that it is not being misused.

Downside risks

Management literature and most chief executives tend to concentrate on how to evaluate the profit potential inherent in any opportunity. That is natural. Positive thinking is the most likely source of positive results, and successful men are generally optimistic by nature.

However, any management decision has more than one potential outcome. It has a downside potential which is only too easy to forget in the excitement of a new venture. In reality, it is usually more important to consider: 'What could we lose by this venture if it goes wrong?', than to consider 'What could we make by it?'.

The massive losses by secondary banks in London in 1974 and 1975 leading to their virtual extinction was caused by their faith in the profit potential of their activities and their optimism. They failed to temper their growth by consideration of the downside potential which finally extinguished them.

It is an important theme of this book that it is the chief executive's job to take risks on behalf of his company. If he does not do so, his company cannot succeed. He is always making risk assessments. His best chance of long-term success lies in avoiding those risks with a large downside potential rather than seizing those with a maximum positive potential.

The quest for knowledge

It is the curse of all hierarchical institutions that promotion to higher positions brings progressive insulation from criticism and challenge even on matters well outside the incumbent's field of knowledge. This often leads to a loss of contact with reality, which is a primary cause of disfunction in large organisations. It also feeds the delusion that there is nothing more to be learned, that past studies and experience have given the man at the top a corpus of knowledge sufficient to last him for the rest of his days. A chief executive would seldom, if ever, say this or even think it. But this attitude may express itself in the fact that he never consciously goes out to search for new understandings.

In truth, learning can never stop. There are obvious reasons for that. First of all nobody can know all the facts even about one area of human endeavour, as witnessed by the constant narrowing of the fields of expertise. Up to 200 years ago, an educated man would move freely from one field of knowledge to another without even recognising the existence of any boundaries between them. As recently as the Victorian age, an engineer like Brunel could break new ground in the design of bridges, ships and machine tools. It probably never occurred to him that civil, marine and mechanical engineering would become distinct professions; but today they are broken down even into more detailed specialised segments.

This subdivision into ever narrower fields of specialisation is, of course, the inevitable outcome of the growth of human knowledge, and in almost every profession a similar pattern has emerged. In medicine, general practitioners rely increasingly on specialist consultants; lawyers specialise in criminal law, company law, divorce, etc.; scientists, architects, accountants all follow the same trend. In addition, new forms of expertise have emerged in recent years, of which sociology is one example. Not only is there a constant expansion of human knowledge, but the world is constantly changing, making old truths obsolete. Relying on the learning of one's youth may result in being left behind in middle-age. To be in the front rank requires a permanent quest for new knowledge.

Two sources of knowledge

The first source of new knowledge lies in the experience gained in working in the environment of the company. This experience needs to be distilled and the only way of doing that is to try to analyse the successes, the failures, the actions of others and one's own doings. It has been said that managers as a group 'are strongly oriented to action and dislike reflective activities'. What I am saying is that only 'reflective activities' can enlarge one's understanding of a business and if there is one manager who has to find the will and the time for them, it is the chief executive.

The second source must be the world around us. The human brain seems to work in mysterious ways. One can never know what it will come up with when stirred by quite unconnected events, experiences or facts. To give it a chance to perform, one must try to imbibe what the external world gives. The chief executive needs to widen his interests — without worrying too much whether all the things he is learning will be of immediate use. To employ a current expression, he must be 'with it'.

By continuing to look at the world in wonder and by reflecting on his experiences in business, he will create antidotes to the affliction of men who wield power: the delusion that their dogmas and prejudices are the acme of human understanding.

The chief executive must have a mite of humility; he must be conscious of the fact that there are things he does not know. And he must never allow himself to become self-satisfied and mentally satiated. He must be thrusting in thought as well as in action.

'Snares and delusions' have not been exhausted in this chapter. People will think of others. To avoid them all is perhaps asking too much for it would require a chief executive with an unlikely mixture of attitudes: humility combined with aggressiveness, caution with optimism, reliance on cold facts with belief in intuition, consistence combined with flexibility, pursuit of excellence combined with a distrust of experts.

The best one can hope for, indeed, the best one can demand, is that a chief executive be aware of the many pitfalls ahead and be on the lookout for others not so clearly perceived. If this is a tall order remember that the chief executive's job is as difficult as it can be exhilarating.

13 Summary

A chief executive's main job is to take the strategic decisions that will determine his company's long-term future. He will not take them in isolation; he will have the support of his executive team and of the company's chairman and part-time directors. But, in the last resort, he must have the policies that he wants, because he is accountable for the results. If things go well he will get the credit but if things go wrong, it will not help him or the company if he says: 'I did not agree with the policy, but I was overruled'. If he disagrees with his colleagues, his choice is between resigning or imposing his decision and seeing it through to whatever outcome emerges. The option of going along with the majority is not one that he should contemplate.

Nevertheless, he still must rely on his executive team to advise him, to implement policies and to manage their own departments. He needs and must exert himself to provide skilled and conscious leadership to that team.

He cannot succeed without taking risks, but he must ensure that those risks are taken after having gathered as much information as possible, and he must positively avoid any situation in which the downside potential is more than he is willing to accept.

The most common failing to be avoided by a chief executive

is over-involvement in short-term, routine activities that divert his attention from the things that really matter. Somehow he must create space in his work programme so that he is not under constant pressure and can sit back and think about his future plans. He must do everthing possible to avoid being in a situation in which he is mainly reacting to pressures rather than initiating events.

He must be able to take a detached view of the battle and avoid getting into the thick of the fight himself even if that is what he enjoys most. Finally, he must remember that success lies not in esoteric techniques or great prescience, but in doing simple things well.

This book, about one of the most important and satisfying jobs in industry, has been written with serious intent. But management can and should be fun. Like every other competitive endeavour there are ups and downs. No one can always be on a winning streak. However, the challenge to do better is always there, so is the pleasure of achievement — and reward for success.

Index

Constraint, freedom from,
    4-5
Consultation:
    and participation contrasted,
        104-5
    as a management style, 100-2
    for decision-making, 104-7
    reasons for success, 100-1
Control, 49-59:
    aspect, select one and
        investigate in depth, 56
    clues, where they come from,
        55
    crucial, deciding what is, 52-3
    getting out and about, 55-7
    of people, 54-7
    overkill technique, 58
    paperwork, 49-50
    performance judging, 54-5
    plans, regular comparisons
        with, 51-3
    progress discussions, 53
    reasons why essential, 50-1
    remedial actions, 57-9
    variance-scanning, 52
    wariness of over-optimism, 50-1
Corporate planning department,
    use of, in strategic
    planning, 28-9
Cost budgets and operational
    planning, 46
Customers:
    maintaining contact with,
        19-20
    wants and needs of, are not
        always the same thing,
        140-1

Decentralisation, 64-5
Decision-making through
    consultation, 104-7
Declining business, reasons for,
    34-5
Defensive planning, 34-6
Delegation aids better judgment
    of subordinate's
    abilities, 64
Deputies, why they are some-
    times promotion
    failures, 2-3
Detail, drugged with, 151-2
Directors:
    relations with non-executive,
        9-10

in boardroom, see Board,
    relations with
Discipline, leader must main-
    tain, 77-9
Diversions from planning
    process, 41-2

Economic factors:
    in strategic planning, 22-3
    trends and operational
        planning, 43-4
Employees need periodic
    reminders of company
    image, 123-4
Equals, system of being first
    among, 97
Example, leadership by good, 78
Executive directors, see Board,
    relations with
Experience, see Knowledge
    and experience
Experts:
    cannot improve position if
        cause is inherent bad
        management, 144
    opinions of, need carefully
        analysing, 143-4
    use of knowledge and
        experience of, 136,
        141-4
    when magic solutions offered,
        look for snags, 158-9

Finance and strategic planning,
    15-16
First among equals principle, 97
Five-year plan, typical
    components of, 29
Forecasts, the point of, 13
Funding and strategic planning,
    29

Grandeur, delusions of, 148-9

Hazards, see Snares and delusions
    under Chief executive
Honesty, there must be
    intellectual, 73-4
House style as sign of company
    image, 126
Humility, aggression and other
    opposites, 162-3

168